# Fantasy World

## Humanity's Avoidance of the Truth to Live in an Illusion

By

## Endall Beall

First Edition

# DEDICATION

This book is dedicated to the real truth seekers, for it is only those who have the unquenchable desire to know who will transcend the illusion.

# Table of Contents

# ACKNOWLEDGEMENTS

I would like to acknowledge my associates Rick and Kat for being there as sounding boards and editors on this project. Your help has been invaluable. My heartfelt thanks.

To my good friend Michel
Rick 10/16/19

# Foreword

This volume has numerous references to articles, videos and .pdf files for expanding and verifying the content of this book. The reader is advised to take advantage of these references in order to gain the most from the material offered in this book.

The author has gone to great lengths to dig out and offer this additional material and provide it within the pages of this book. To gain the greatest advantage of this presentation it behooves the reader to capitalize on this additional information. This supporting information is compiled and provided as a launching point for deeper investigative research. The reader has at their disposal, with all this additional material, the capability to gain a world of insights and information if they will take the time to investigate all that is presented herein. To do less will only leave the reader lacking in knowledge and walking away from the experience of reading this book with less perceptual understanding.

The material in this book is offered for the benefit of the reader. The author is already intimately aware of these things and more and had no real obligation to unearth and share any of this information except for the benefit of the reader. We ask that you use all the material in this book wisely.

# Introduction

Here is the truth – you are at war and you don't even know it. No one bothered to inform you that you are at war, so you remain blissfully ignorant of the fact that you are targeted in this war. You live an illusion where you are distracted with your daily jobs or routines, seeking refuge from the workday through escapist avenues like sports, the little league games, the daughter's dance recitals, the visit to Disneyland or whatever other amusement park you may frequent, getting lost in meaningless TV episodes of escapist reality and so on. All these things were intentionally designed to keep your attention distracted from the hard fact that you are at war, and that this war has been subversively waged against you for over a century.

There was no public declaration of this war because those who are targeted may have had the chance to prepare themselves and fight back. The perpetrators of this war have been the elite intellectual classes who push the idea of Globalism through embracing communist ideologies as fellow travelers to the agenda put forth by the Communist International and secret societies like the Freemasons and, more notably, the British Fabian Society and its diverse web of NGOs and other extra-governmental organizations.

The immediate response by most of the public apprised of these facts will be denial. This is how deeply the psychological conditioning controls the public mind. This is a war for your mind above all else. There have been no bullets and bombs used in this war because the mind is the battlefield. Make no mistake, all the wars that have been fought throughout the 20th century have been part of this war, but without the subversive psychological manipulation, humanity may have avoided most of these wars.

This has been a war of propaganda, intentional omission of historical facts, and a wealth of disinformation about what people perceive as their national history. The world has been duped into digesting lie after lie and believing it all as truth. This is the illusion which humanity lives and, generally speaking, the lies are more comfortable to accept than the truth. If one accepts the truth they become responsible for their own well-being.

There are millions of people all around the world who are finally starting to awaken themselves from the seductive lies of the illusion they think is reality, but the illusion runs deep and is more ancient than the public would prefer to believe. The fact is that our entire perceptual reality is based on lies and sleight of hand illusions intentionally fostered by those whose only goal is to drive the majority of humanity into slavery and destitution.

There have been warnings and clarion calls to awaken the public at large by many authors over the last century, but their voices have either been silenced or their messages disparaged by those who have a vested interest in keeping this subversive war for global domination moving inexorably forward.

The world is controlled by elite factions of a criminal cabal that make the Mafia look like pikers in comparison. At least within the Mafia there is an internal code of honor that is not present in the globalist communist cabal that seeks total control of the planet. Through silent and patient subversion, what the Fabian Society calls gradualist Marxism, the world has been put to sleep, caught in a spell whereby the illusion is more enchanting than the truth they intentionally hide from the public. This book is but one more attempt by this author to reveal this illusion which runs deep and pervasive in every belief we embrace, and that includes religious and spiritual beliefs. I have devoted tens of thousands of words providing what I feel is irrefutable evidence for my assertions in my books. But who takes the time to read anymore? Who cares enough to discover the truth compared to all those wrapped up in their ego illusions taking selfies and believing in their own self-importance so much that they share these stupid images with the world through social media outlets?

Through control of most publishing houses, the truth rarely gets out to the public. If it does happen to sneak through, rest assured that globalist sympathizers within academia or the political arena will soon seek to destroy the messenger in an attempt to destroy the messages of truth that are being aired more by the week.

Truth shatters the illusion, but the fact is that most people are simply too psychologically weak to handle facing the truth. They prefer the illusion because it makes them 'feel good', and sadly, feeling good is more important than feeling strong and informed. The world stands on the precipice of psychological destruction and humanity is utterly clueless about its plight in the face of living the illusions it embraces as its reality. Escapism is more important than being cognitively armed to combat the enemy in this battlefield for your consciousness.

While people worry about some form of mind-control devices waiting in the wings, the fact is that the public worldwide is already so mind-controlled that they will deny the fact that they are. *You* are mind controlled and will want to punch me in the face for insisting on this truth. That is as it should be, for all mind-controlled slaves will fight to defend their illusions rather than face harsh truth. No matter who you are or what you believe, someone holds the leash on your consciousness and leads you where *they* want you to go. There is no better slave than one who believes they are free. The illusion exercises great power over human consciousness and this control goes back thousands of years. With the advent of the field of psychology, the elite have public mind-control techniques down to a science, and humanity remains none the wiser today than our ancestors did when the same tactics were used on them. The question that is foremost for every reader is whether they want to break free of this cognitive slavery or continue to embrace the illusion. This is the ultimate choice at its most basic level.

# 1. Communism is Not Dead

Contrary to some perceptions in the West, communism did not die when the Berlin Wall came down and the Marxist Socialist ideology finally failed in the old Soviet Union. Many in the world breathed a selective sigh of relief when the Iron Curtain came down, falsely believing that at the end of the Cold War with Russia, the world was once again safe from the communist menace. How could any critically thinking individual fall for such a ruse when Communist China was still a major power in the Far East? How could we believe that communism was dead while Marxist Jesuits and other elite Leftists kept building communist regimes in South and Central America? The fact is that communism is not dead. It has had a very long and fateful existence of economic failures, murdering hundreds of millions over the decades as its plan for global domination moved inexorably forward.

Communism succeeds through subversion and controlling ideas through the manipulation of language. It no longer calls itself communism in most circles, it is now called Socialism, or Progressivism, Political Correctness, or even worse – Social Justice. Modern communism hides behind many verbal masks in order to keep its murderous ideology hidden from the public. The abuse and manipulation of language is one of its greatest tools of deception through propaganda.

Through the manipulation of words, phrases and language, the communists and their fellow travelers in the media lull the public into a form of soft brainwashing. Their elitist academic think tanks work tirelessly to develop these terms and then saturate the public consciousness with them through its controlled media outlets and the TV and film industry.

Although the Russian communist empire has crumbled, the Chinese Communists have quickly filled the void formerly controlled by the Russian communists on American soil. Through collusion with the British Fabian Society, who I personally feel has been coordinating these communist efforts since its creation in 1884, first Russia, and now China are following in the footsteps of their Fabian masters as merely the front organizations to hide who is really running the show in the globalist arena.

As the former British PM Margaret Thatcher astutely articulated, "The trouble with socialism is that eventually you run out of other people's money". Communism would not be alive today were it not for the perfidious infusion of cash from rich Western nations who supported communism over the last 100 years while claiming to be at war against communism. As much as Americans may wish to argue the point, there is plenty of easily verifiable evidence that supports this fact. In recent decades, were it not for U.S. politicians favoring China in its trade practices, China would not have had the money to build its modern military. This is no different than U.S. politicians since the administration of Woodrow Wilson onward who sustained Russia with U.S. taxpayer dollars to prop up the murderous communist regimes of the Bolsheviks, and later, Stalin.

What must be noted before I proceed in this chapter is that present day communism finds its roots with a specific group of people in Russia, yet today the communist ideologues come in all races and sexes worldwide. What follows is not a condemnation of any race of people as a whole, but a condemnation of certain bad apples who embraced the ideology of communism and used it to push forward their own avaricious and criminal tyrannical agenda. Every race of human beings on this planet has their latent tyrants and abusers. The facts I am about to share are not a condemnation of the Jewish people as a whole, but is a condemnation of those who embraced and executed the communist ideology in the Soviet Union. Remember, we are talking about bad apples – a global criminal cabal. This has nothing to do with race and everything to do with communist criminal enterprises across the globe

Coupled with communism is world Zionism. Based on the writings of Jewish communists themselves, the world Zionist movement is intimately interwoven with the communist agenda for global domination. For those Christians who believe that the creation of the State of Israel was a prophetic occurrence, you have really had the wool pulled over your eyes. The following quotes come from the perpetrators themselves. Read and learn

*"Communism and internationalism are in*

*truth and in fact great virtues. Judaism may be justly proud of these virtues"*

Harry Waton, A Program for the Jews and an Answer to All Anti-Semites (New York: Committee for the Preservation of the Jews, 1939), p. 80"

*"If the tide of history does not turn toward Communist internationalism ... then the Jewish race is doomed."*

George Marlen, Stalin, Trotsky, or Lenin (New York, 1937), p. 414

*"The [Jewish] Commissaries were formerly political exiles. They had been dreaming of revolution for years in their exile in Paris, in London, in New York, in Berlin, everywhere and anywhere. They saw in the Bolshevist Movement an opportunity of realizing the extreme ideas of Communism and internationalism to which their fate had compelled them."*

Dr. D. S. Pazmanik, in The Jewish Chronicle (London), September 5, 1919, p. 14

*"The Jewish people will never forget that the Soviet Union was the first country - and as yet*

*the only country in the world - in which anti-Semitism is a crime.*"

Jewish Voice (New York: National Council of Jewish Communists), January 1942, p. 16

*"Anti-Semitism was classed [by the Soviet Government] as counter-revolution and the severe punishments meted out for acts of anti-Semitism were the means by which the existing order protected its own safety"*

The Congress Bulletin, (New York: American Jewish Congress), January 5, 1940, p. 2

*"Anti-Communism is anti-Semitism."*

Jewish Voice (New York: National Council of Jewish Communists), July-August 1941, p. 23

*"The part which Jews play in the [Communist] Government of the country [Russia] does not appear to be declining"*

Harry Sacher, in The Jewish Review (London), June-August 1932, p. 43

*"The Russian intelligentsia . . . saw in the philosophy of Judaism the germs of Bolshevism –*

11

*the struggle of ... Judaism versus Christianity."*

Leon Dennen, in The Menorah Journal (New York, July-September 1932, p. 105

*"Russian Jews have taken a prominent part in the Bolshevist movement"*

The American Hebrew (New York), November 18, 1927, p. 20

*"Jewry has come to wield a considerable power in the Communist Party."*

Dr. Avrahm Yarmolinsky, in The Menorah Journal (New York), July 1928, p. 37

*"It is not an accident that Judaism gave birth to Marxism, and it is not an accident that the Jews readily took up Marxism; all this is in perfect accord with the progress of Judaism and the Jews."*

Harry Waton, A Program for the Jews and an Answer to All Anti-Semites (New York: Committee for the Preservation of the Jews, 1939), p. 148

*"There are many Bolshevik leaders of Jewish extraction."*

D. L. Sandelsan, in The Jewish Chronicle

These are the words of Jewish communists themselves arrogantly professing their agenda to the world. I didn't make them up. How much of this truth was taught you about the communists in your history classes? And this is just a small smattering of these truths that abound if one does the research into who was behind one of the most murderous regimes in human history. The greatest singular mass murderer in history was not Adolph Hitler, but a Jewish communist named Lazar Kaganovich who is singularly responsible for the Ukrainian Holodomor, where it is calculated that he intentionally starved between 10-30 million people. Hitler's alleged 6 million looks paltry in comparison.

Overall, communist regimes are guilty of the murder and extermination of between 150-300 million human beings worldwide since the Bolshevik Revolution, yet you rarely hear these numbers, or see reports about the communist crimes committed in history books or through mainstream TV and movies. This is the ugly secret that must be continually swept under the rug of falsely reported and intentionally sanitized history. This ugly secret is why we have Hitler and his 6 million victims shoved down our throat day after day virtually everywhere we turn. So long as the communist Globalists can keep the public mind glued on the crimes of Hitler, they can continue to whitewash the greater crimes of communism over the last century.

By providing the foregoing evidence I am not condemning a race as there are many Jews who are patriotic Americans and who are not communists. I am not here to condemn an entire race for the actions of criminals of their race. I am not anti-Semitic; I am anti-tyranny. If Jews are tyrants in their murderous communist actions, then I have a problem with those tyrants, regardless of their race. I harbor no ill will for other Jews who are not a part of that tyranny. I am not a racist.

Communist ideology goes back thousands of years and can be found in the so-called Essene community at Qumran, which also has similar aspects with Freemasonry in its rites and rituals. A form of communism was also found in early Christian colonies. The Roman Empire was a form of socialism whereby the general population was given bread and/or grain by the government. Whenever the Emperor couldn't supply this bread to the people, revolts soon followed.

Historically, nothing happens in a vacuum. Although we are bombarded almost daily in the West about the atrocities of Hitler (and I am by no means giving Hitler any kind of free pass as he was just another murderous tyrant), the international community of Jewry declared war on Germany publicly in 1933. See *Anti-Nazi Boycott of 1933* at Wikipedia.

https://en.wikipedia.org/wiki/Anti-Nazi_boycott_of_1933

What goes unreported in all the propaganda against Hitler is that the Jews were not blameless in what Hitler did with the Holocaust. Jewish communists had formed the first Antifa group in 1932-1933. As Wikipedia reports under *Antifa (Germany)*:

*"Antifaschistische Aktion (German: [ˌantifaˈʃɪstɪʃə ʔakˈtsi̯oːn]), commonly known under its abbreviation Antifa (German: [ˈantifaː]),* **was an organisation affiliated with the Communist Party of Germany (KPD)** *that existed from 1932 to 1933.*

*Under the leadership of Ernst Thälmann, the KPD had become a staunchly Stalinist party, and it had been largely controlled and funded by the Soviet leadership since 1928; the party had adopted the position that it was "the only anti-fascist party" while it regarded all other parties, and especially the Social Democratic Party (SPD), as "fascists." The KPD did not view "fascism" as a specific political movement, but primarily as the final stage of capitalism, and "anti-fascism" was therefore synonymous with anti-capitalism. The KPD stated that "fighting fascism means fighting the SPD just as much as it means fighting Hitler and the parties of Brüning." In 1929 the KPD's paramilitary group Roter Frontkämpferbund was banned as extremist by the governing social democrats. The Antifaschistische Aktion was formed largely as a counter-move to the social democrats' establishment of the Iron Front in*

15

*1931, which the KPD regarded as a "social fascist terror organisation." The Antifaschistische Aktion was an integral part of the KPD and was mainly active as a KPD campaign during the elections in 1932. During its brief existence the Antifaschistische Aktion focused in large part on attacking the social democrats, as they were seen by the KPD as the most dangerous and capable fascists; the KPD viewed the Nazi Party as a less sophisticated fascist party and as the lesser evil compared to the SPD, and sometimes cooperated with them in attacking the social democrats."*

This is the communist origin of Antifa and is the father of the same movement in America and worldwide today. What we are seeing on U.S. soil with the revival of this communist terrorist group is just a replay of history. As the passages cited note, it is not about white supremacy as much as it is about anti-capitalism — communism's sworn enemy.

While the communist operatives in the CIA-controlled Mockingbird press give Antifa a free pass and spew their swill about President Donald Trump being a fascist, we are seeing the same issue that Hitler faced from the communists, who were mostly Jews, in Germany in the 1930s. This is not anti-Semitism; it is historical fact that has been intentionally whitewashed in the West so the Communist International can creep into Western culture to eventually undermine it. Sadly, they have been very successful in covering up these facts to date. We are only watching a rerun of history on U.S. soil today, and most Americans are utterly clueless where it all began or what is behind it. This is evidenced by people calling Antifa Fascists in their ignorance, not knowing they are and always have been communists.

As in the U.S. today, the Jewish population in Russia was about 3%, yet when the communists came to power bringing in their decades long reign of terror, Jewish operatives controlled at least 40% of the political establishment. Although many Russians were compelled to toe the party line out of fear of execution or going to the Gulags, it was still the Jewish communist leadership who were themselves the most complicit in dictating the murderous policies implemented under communist domination.

Despite what some may believe, the push for global domination is not strictly a Jewish plan. Although they have been highly instrumental in pushing the communist globalist agenda, they have had plenty of support over the past few centuries by other power-hungry elitists from different races. These elite factions I refer to specifically as the Aryans.

Contrary to popular belief, the Aryan races are not all White. I have shown in my prior works that the Aryan overlords, those who feel they are ultimately suited and destined to rule all humanity, come from many racial variants. Where people compartmentalize their perceptions of history, buying the historical propaganda of the times, I have seen few scholars who have correlated the similarities of the Aryan breed over the ages and seen them for what they are. If you look at Genghis Khan, the

Roman Emperors, Napoleon, Alexander the Great, Adolph Hitler, Mao Tse Tung and the Communist regimes and compare them, you will find the same pattern of murder and terrorism throughout the ages. Every one of these presumed world conquerors stooped to the same level of murderous depravity, regardless of the ideology of their times. They were all murderers and terrorists and ruled with iron fists. They were all cut from the same mold. We find the same pattern in the Persian conquests, the expansion of Roman Catholicism and its Inquisitions and the expansion of the Ottoman empire. Slaughter is the name of the game to these Aryan monsters, and the more adversaries slaughtered, the more they reveled in their glory.

There is no difference between Genghis Khan, Lenin and Stalin than there is with an Idi Amin and a Pol Pot. Some leave a larger train of murders behind them than others, but the communist ideology in modern times is only a new label on an old brand of Aryan tyranny. Modern communists in the U.S. today have hidden behind the mask of academia and the burgeoning bureaucratic state. Through slow subversion and brainwashing the public through controlling the flow of valid information, Western populations have been lulled into a state of complacency by placing trust in individuals and institutions who deserve no such trust.

In America today the barbarians are not at the gate, they are in the house, and the greater public is blissfully unaware of where their culture went through the erosive gradualist form of communism sponsored by the British Fabian Society. The lion's share of scholars, academics and psychologists have been fellow travelers to the communist agenda. Psychology has been used as a *weapon* and was never any kind of healing art. Psychology cures *nothing*. Through selling the public a false image of psychology, millions are now dependent on psychoactive drugs legitimately doled out by psychologists who are merely drug pimps for the pharmaceutical companies. The same can be said for half the practicing doctors in the healthcare profession.

With the advent of technology, along with psychological manipulation through controlling the flow of information, we are now faced with frequency control through technologies developed by Hendricus G. Loos, what I refer to as the Loos devices. Through television, radio and the internet, electromagnetic frequencies are transmitted through electronic media to trigger the human central nervous system in order to generate specific emotional reactions. I covered this in depth in my book *Emotionalism: How the Human Herds are Controlled*. I highly recommend that the reader peruse these patents issued by the U.S. government to Mr. Loos if you doubt the veracity of what I am telling you. Just look up *'Patents by Hendricus G. Loos'* to see these patents at the U.S. Patent Office website. Link below for Kindle readers.

https://patents.justia.com/inventor/hendricus-g-loos

The communist psychologists learned long ago that in order to generate a psychological response in an unwary public, one must first engage their emotions. This is why we see such emotional fervor in the modern leftist movements around the world. There is no thinking present in the adherents to the hoax Global Warming Green Agenda, only raw emotions. The same can be said of Antifa and its over-emotional followers. If you want to see psychological brainwashing in its most extreme action, just look around you.

Using the Jewish Communist model, as quoted previously, the Globalist communists are at war against Christianity. Islam is already a religion based on submission. In fact, Islam means submission when translated into English. It is already a religion of regimented thought and zealotry. Up until the time of the Protestant Revolution, spawned by the Rosicrucian Martin Luther, the same type of zealotry exhibited in Islam was prevalent in Roman Catholicism. What modern Christians don't realize about their whitewashed religious stories is that, just as the communists seek to destroy the past so they can write their own future doctrines, the Christians got there first over 1,700 years ago.

While Christians are lost in the idealized stories about Jesus and his miracles, coupled with presumed prophecy, in its early days Christianity was comprised of mobs of zealots destroying the Pagan past so they could rewrite a Christian future. This is verifiable historical fact, not fiction, and the churches have all decided to remove these episodes of Christian zealot mob destruction from their pulpits, either preaching fire and brimstone and the coming tribulation, or pushing a false sense of compassion and humanitarianism to earn one's way to heaven. You are not taught about the book burnings ordered by the Emperor Constantine to eradicate any and all Pagan writings that disagreed with the new Roman Catholic Christian narrative, yet these book-burning orders are historically verifiable.

The controlled mainstream news outlets refuse to report that the influx of illegal aliens from at least 60 different countries around the world invading the U.S. from the Latin American countries, is financed by communist-supported agencies working in direct collusion and cooperation with Marxist Jesuits, who have been preaching revolution in South and Central America since the 1950s. This Marxist Jesuit doctrine is called *Liberation Theology*. Wikipedia describe this in part this way:

> *"Liberation theology is a synthesis of Christian theology and Marxist socio-economic analyses that emphasizes social concern for the poor and political liberation for oppressed peoples. In the 1950s and the 1960s, liberation theology was the political praxis of Latin American theologians, such as Gustavo Gutiérrez of Peru, Leonardo Boff of Brazil, Juan Luis Segundo of Uruguay, and Jon Sobrino of Spain, who popularized the phrase "Preferential option for the poor".*

> *The Latin American context also produced evangelical advocates of liberation theology, such*

*as C. René Padilla of Ecuador, Samuel Escobar of Peru, and Orlando E. Costas of Puerto Rico, who, in the 1970s, called for integral mission, emphasizing evangelism and social responsibility.*

*Theologies of liberation have developed in other parts of the world such as black theology in the United States and South Africa, Palestinian liberation theology, Dalit theology in India, and Minjung theology in South Korea."*

*"The best-known form of liberation theology is that which developed within the Catholic Church in Latin America in the 1950s and 1960s, arising principally as a moral reaction to the poverty and social injustice in the region. The term was coined in 1971 by the Peruvian priest Gustavo Gutiérrez, who wrote one of the movement's defining books, A Theology of Liberation. Other noted exponents include Leonardo Boff of Brazil, Jon Sobrino of Spain, and Juan Luis Segundo of Uruguay.*

*Latin American liberation theology met opposition in the United States, which accused it of using "Marxist concepts", and led to admonishment by the Vatican's Congregation for the Doctrine of the Faith (CDF) in 1984 and 1986. While stating that "in itself, the expression "theology of liberation" is a thoroughly valid term", The Vatican rejected certain forms of Latin American liberation theology for focusing on institutionalized or systemic sin and for identifying Catholic Church hierarchy in South America as members of the same privileged class that had long been oppressing indigenous populations from the arrival of Pizarro onward."*

As noted, these concepts of Marxist ideology have infiltrated into Western churches, even evangelical churches, hiding behind the mask of Christian Zionism. Regarding *Christian Zionism*, Wikipedia reports in part:

*"Christian Zionism is a belief among some Christians that the return of the Jews to the Holy Land and the establishment of the state of Israel in 1948 were in accordance with Bible prophecy. The term began to be used in the mid-20th century, superseding Christian Restorationism.*

*However, Christian advocacy grew after the Protestant Reformation in support of the restoration of the Jews and has its roots "in seventeenth century England". A contemporary*

*Israeli historian suggests that evangelical Christian Zionists in England of the 1840s "passed this notion on to Jewish circles", while Jewish nationalism in the early 19th century was widely regarded with hostility by British Jews.*

*Some Christian Zionists believe that the gathering of the Jews in Israel is a prerequisite for the Second Coming of Jesus. The idea has been common in Protestant circles since the Reformation that Christians should actively support a Jewish return to the Land of Israel, along with the parallel idea that the Jews ought to be encouraged to become Christians as a means of fulfilling Biblical prophecy."*

It should be noted that the terminology Christian Zionism made its way into the American Christian lexicon prior to the establishment of the State of Israel in 1948. It was all a psychological setup. By convincing Christians that the return of the Jews to Israel was part of Bible prophecy, American Christians in particular, were hoodwinked into allowing Jewish Marxist terrorists to invade and take over the land of Palestine (which was under Syrian control at the time). Look up *Irgun* and the *Stern Gang* on Wikipedia for more.

The concept of Christian Zionism was a deliberately formulated psychological manipulation preying on Christian hopes that if the Jews returned to the Holy Land that the Second Coming was close at hand. It was all a psychological con game, and still is. For an excellent example of fantasy world bubble busting about Christian Zionism, I direct the reader to an article entitled, *Why Everything You Think You Know About Christian Zionism Is Wrong* by Raphael Magarik. For Kindle readers find the link to this article below.

https://forward.com/culture/430251/why-everything-you-think-you-know-about-christian-zionism-is-wrong/

The problem with living in the fantasy world of superficial beliefs and illusions is that facts have a very unpleasant way of busting those bubbles of illusion. Naturally, on the psychological level, in order to avoid cognitive discomfort from facing the truths that unmask the illusions, denial and irrational reasoning (apologetics) are always close at hand. The mind will go to any lengths it can to avoid cognitive dissonance. Cognitive dissonance occurs when we believe one thing and actual truth exposes the belief as a superficial lie or set of lies. To preserve our psychological equilibrium (cognitive resonance) we will resort to lying to ourselves to preserve the belief in the presence of hard, truthful facts to the contrary – or we simply deny the truth so we can continue to embrace the illusion. Even though the cognitive illusion may be wholly false, it makes us feel psychologically comfortable to continue to embrace the lie over the truth.

The communists have read your Bible. They understand the psychology of beliefs, and they know exactly how to manipulate you with your own belief in alleged prophecy to fulfill their dastardly agenda. To be naïve enough to not realize this is also a failure of the superficial illusionary belief bubbles we embrace over facing the hard truth, i.e. we don't *believe* we can have our minds manipulated in such a crass fashion. We don't lie to any other person more than we lie to ourselves, and the communist psychologists are fully aware of this human failing, which they exploit to the maximum to control your consciousness. In the fantasy world, your mind is putty in the hands of professional psychological manipulators. This is hard truth and easily proven, which I did in my book, *The Psychology of Becoming Human: Evolving Beyond Psychological Conditioning.*

# 2. All Major Religions Have Bloody Hands

If one listens to religious adherents of any kind, they all profess a religion of love or peace without exception. Regardless of this comfortable cognitive lie the followers of the major world religions profess, every one of them has blood on their hands. Among these religions we must also count Marxism, which by Jewish admission, as noted in the previous chapter, is Judaism secularized into worshipping the State as God. The psychologists Gustave le Bon proved the religious nature of Socialism in his book *The Psychology of Socialism*. It is a volume I highly suggest reading if anyone wants to understand the beast called Socialism. This book can be found in pdf format for free online at archive.org at the link below:

https://archive.org/details/psychologysocia00bongoog/page/n7

I am going to start with Christianity in this analysis because it will probably primarily be read by a Western audience. By starting with Christianity, the reader should in no way presume that I am targeting Christian violence above any other religious violence. All things are equal in this presentation and one must start somewhere. There is no justification to the murder and mayhem wrought by *any* religion. If we look up *European Wars of Religion* on Wikipedia we find in part:

> *"With minor exceptions, the Thirty Years' War marked the end of trumpeting Christianity as the major motivation for mass-scale murder. According to Voltaire in his listing of "Christian barbarities", Christianity, from the sacrifice of Jesus up to 1769, was responsible for 9,468,800 deaths. A more popular figure from 1897 by* The Rationalist's Manual *by M. D. Aletheia gave a death toll of 56 million:*

> *Let us look for a moment at the number of victims sacrificed on the altars of the Christian Moloch: 1,000,000 perished during the early Arian schism; 1,000,000 during the Carthaginian struggle; 7,000,000 during the Saracen slaughters in Spain. 5,000,000 perished during the eight Crusades; 2,000,000 of Saxons and Scandinavians lost their lives in opposing the introduction of the blessings of Christianity. 1,000,000 were destroyed in the Holy(?) Wars against the Netherlands, Albigenses, Waldenses, and Huguenots. 30,000,000 Mexicans and Peruvians were slaughtered before they could be convinced*

*of the beauties(?) of the Christian creed. 9,000,000*
*were burned for witchcraft. Total,* **56,000,000.***"*

From the website below, called Political Islam, we get the
following death counts in an article entitled *Tears of Jihad*:

https://www.politicalislam.com/tears-of-jihad/

Africa – 120,000,000
Christians – 60,000,000
Hindus – 80,000,000
Buddhists – 10,000,000

Jews capitulated to Muslim demands and wound up
serving their Muslim masters, so the Jewish death count (of
thousands) is inconsequential in comparison to the tens of millions
according to this article. The grand total of deaths by Jihad and
the African slave trade brings the total to 270,000,000 deaths by
Islam.

It is harder to find the overall death toll for Hinduism, but
a 2017 report of 198 world religions finds Hinduism the 4th worse
religion for intolerance, trailing behind Syria, Nigeria and Iraq
respectively reported at Quartz India in the article *India is the
fourth-worst country in the world for religious violence,* which
can be found at the link below:

For more information on Hinduism see *Religious Violence in India* at Wikipedia.

Now we are going to go where most people will be surprised, and that is Buddhism. The West has been sold the image of the peaceful smiling Buddhist monk, and few would believe that Buddhism also has its own bloody history. The following excerpts come from *Buddhism and Violence* at Wikipedia:

> *"The relationship between Buddhism and violence includes acts of violence and aggression committed by Buddhists with religious, political, or socio-cultural motivations, as well as self-inflicted violence by ascetics or for religious purposes. Buddhism is generally seen as among the religious traditions least associated with violence. However, in the history of Buddhism, there have been acts of violence directed, promoted, or inspired by Buddhists. As far as Buddha's teachings and scriptures are concerned, Buddhism forbids violence for resolving conflicts."*

> *"In Southeast Asia, Thailand has had several prominent virulent Buddhist monastic calls*

*for violence. In the 1970s, nationalist Buddhist monks like Phra Kittiwuttho argued that killing Communists did not violate any of the Buddhist precepts. The militant side of Thai Buddhism became prominent again in 2004 when a Malay Muslim insurgency renewed in Thailand's deep south. At first Buddhist monks ignored the conflict as they viewed it as political and not religious but eventually they adopted an "identity-formation", as practical realities require deviations from religious ideals."*

*"Buddhism in Sri Lanka has a unique history and has played an important role in the shaping of Sinhalese nationalist identity. Consequently, politicized Buddhism has contributed to ethnic tension in the island between the majority Sinhalese Buddhist population and other minorities, especially the Tamils."*

*"With the rise of modern Sinhalese Buddhist nationalism in the late nineteenth and early twentieth centuries as a reaction to the changes brought under the British colonialism, the old religious mytho-history of the Mahavamsa (especially the emphasis on the Sinhalese and Tamil ethnicities of Duthagamani and Elara,*

*respectively) was revitalized and consequently would prove to be detrimental to the intergroup harmony in the island. As Heather Selma Gregg writes: "Modern-day Sinhalese nationalism, rooted in local myths of being a religiously chosen people and of special progeny, demonstrates that even a religion perceived as inherently peaceful can help fuel violence and hatred in its name."*

*Buddhist revivalism took place among the Sinhalese to counter Christian missionary influence. The British commissioned the Sinhala translation of the Mahavamsa (which was originally written in Pali), thereby making it accessible to the wider Sinhalese population. During this time the first riot in modern Sri Lankan history broke out in 1883, between Buddhists and Catholics, highlighting the "growing religious divide between the two communities".*

*"Other minority groups have also come under attack by Sinhalese Buddhist nationalists. Fear of country's Buddhist hegemony being challenged by Christian proselytism has driven Buddhist monks and organizations to demonize Christian organizations with one popular monk comparing missionary activity to terrorism; as a*

*result, Sinhalese Buddhist nationalists, including the JVP and JHU, who oppose attempts to convert Buddhists to another religion, support or conduct anti-Christian violence. The number of attacks against Christian churches rose from 14 in 2000 to over 100 in 2003. Dozens of these acts were confirmed by U.S. diplomatic observers. This anti-Christian violence was led by extremist Buddhist clergy and has included acts of "beatings, arson, acts of sacrilege, death threats, violent disruption of worship, stoning, abuse, unlawful restraint, and even interference with funerals". It has been noted that the strongest anti-West sentiments accompany the anti-Christian violence since the Sinhalese Buddhist nationalists identify Christianity with the West which they think is conspiring to undermine Buddhism.]*

*In the postwar Sri Lanka, ethnic and religious minorities continue face threat from Sinhalese Buddhist nationalism. There have been continued sporadic attacks on Christian churches by Buddhist extremists who allege Christians of conducting unethical or forced conversion. The Pew Research Center has listed Sri Lanka among the countries with very high religious hostilities in 2012 due to the violence committed by Buddhist monks against Muslim and Christian places of worship. These acts included attacking a mosque and forcefully taking over a Seventh-day advent church and converting it into a Buddhist temple.*

*Extremist Buddhist leaders justify their attacks on the places of worship of minorities by arguing that Sri Lanka is the promised land of the Sinhalese Buddhists to safeguard Buddhism. The recently formed Buddhist extremist group, the Bodu Bala Sena (BBS), or Buddhist Power Force, founded by Buddhist monks in 2012, has been accused of inciting the anti-Muslim riots that killed 4 Muslims and injured 80 in 2014. The leader of the BBS, in linking the government's military victory over the LTTE to the ancient Buddhist king conquest of Tamil king Elara, said that Tamils have been taught a lesson twice and warned other minorities of the same fate if they tried to challenge Sinhalese Buddhist culture."*

*"The beginning of "Buddhist violence" in Japan relates to a long history of feuds among Buddhists. The sōhei or "warrior monks" appeared during the Heian period, although the seeming contradiction in being a Buddhist "warrior monk" caused controversy even at the time. More directly*

*linked is that the Ikkō-shū movement was considered an inspiration to Buddhists in the Ikkō-ikki rebellion. In Osaka they defended their temple with the slogan "The mercy of Buddha should be recompensed even by pounding flesh to pieces. One's obligation to the Teacher should be recompensed even by smashing bones to bits!"*

*During World War II, Japanese Buddhist literature from that time, as part of its support of the Japanese war effort, stated "In order to establish eternal peace in East Asia, arousing the great benevolence and compassion of Buddhism, we are sometimes accepting and sometimes forceful. We now have no choice but to exercise the benevolent forcefulness of 'killing one in order that many may live' (issatsu tashō). This is something which Mahayana Buddhism approves of only with the greatest of seriousness..." Almost all Japanese Buddhists temples strongly supported Japan's militarization."*

I think this is enough information to explode that bubble of illusion about the peaceful smiling Buddhist monks. The Dalai Lama, who is the head of world Buddhism and holds a position within that religion the same as the Pope to Catholics, is a self-professed Marxist. In the short video link below on YouTube entitled, *"Dalai Lama, "I prefer Socialism, I am a Marxist",* you can hear the words straight from the horse's mouth so to speak.

https://www.youtube.com/watch?v=DhvlnC-oKEw&t=22s

This is only one example of the Dalai Lama making these statements. There are other selections on YouTube if you want to hear it more than once on other occasions.

It should also be noted that Pope Francis is the first Jesuit Pope in the history of the Catholic Church. He is from Argentina, a hotbed of Marxist Liberation Theology, and is also a Marxist in his ideological perspective, although he has not plainly admitted such to his congregation or he would most likely be ousted.

The point in bringing the information in this chapter forward is to illustrate how religious ideologies of all kinds are willing to go to no end of violence to enforce their faith, discriminate against opposing religionists through threat, coercion, arson, murder, riots and generally causing mayhem. To the 270,000,000 previously cited, we can add about 40,000,000 deaths from WW I and about 70-85 million in WW II, many of whom died believing they were defending God and country in their efforts to defeat the Kaiser in WW I and Hitler, Japan and Italy in WW II. Of course, the Germans and Italians also thought they were fighting on the side of the same God in many cases. Although these two World Wars were not fought as religious wars, religion played a major role in the mindset of many soldiers. As the adage goes, "There are no Atheists in a foxhole."

The Jesuit Order was created by Ignatius Loyola, a Portuguese soldier whose leg was wounded by cannon fire and who, while in convalescence prayed for guidance. According to Loyola he was delivered 'visions', allegedly by Mary, the mother of Christ. Through these visions Loyola dedicated himself to the Queen of Heaven and developed his exercises and practices for strict adherence and means for converting the mind of a child to the Catholic faith for life. In other words, he developed a manner of psychological conditioning through which the Church could control its membership.

The Mariolatry of the Catholic Church is no less than ancient Mother Goddess worship wrapped in the trappings of Christian Catholicism. The worship of the Mother Mary as the Queen of Heaven is merely a pastiche of former Pagan Mother Goddesses from the ancient past grafted onto Catholic dogma. I provided a wealth of evidence to support this claim in my book *Gutting Mysticism: Explaining the Roots of all Supernatural Beliefs*.

Loyola was a *converso*, or *morano* – a Jew who had converted to Catholicism. Through the avenue of political intrigues, the Jesuit Order, or Society of Jesus as it is called, was banned in many European countries over continual political intrigues. Under *Suppression of the Society of Jesus* at Wikipedia we find in part:

*"Prior to the eighteenth-century suppression of the Jesuits in many countries, there was an early ban in territories of the Venetian Republic between 1606 and 1656/7, begun and ended as part of disputes between the Republic and the Papacy, beginning with the Venetian Interdict.*

*By the mid-18th century, the Society had acquired a reputation in Europe for political maneuvering and economic success. Monarchs in many European states grew progressively wary of what they saw as undue interference from a foreign entity. The expulsion of Jesuits from their states had the added benefit of allowing governments to impound the Society's accumulated wealth and possessions. However, historian Charles Gibson cautions, "[h]ow far this served as a motive for the expulsion we do not know.""*

It is reported through some sources that the Jesuit Order is the largest intelligence gathering organization on the planet. Given the nature of the confessional, this is not hard to accept as fact given how widespread the Order is around the planet in every country, and it also explains how Jesuit intrigues within royal courts often led to wars at their instigation, not to mention the reason for the expulsion of the Order from many European nations.

So far we have shown that two of the leaders of two major world religions are Marxists. I have shown the deep connection between Marxism and Christian Zionism which reaches into many Protestant evangelical churches, many of them having very large congregations and being very rich (see your favorite televangelist). So, now let's look at Islam and see if we can find similar connections. If we look up *Islamic Socialism* at Wikipedia we find:

> *"Islamic socialism is a term coined by various Muslim leaders to describe a more spiritual form of socialism. Muslim socialists believe that the teachings of the Quran and Muhammad—especially the zakat—are compatible with principles of economic and social equality. They draw inspiration from the early Medinan welfare state established by Muhammad. Muslim socialists found their roots in anti-imperialism. Muslim socialist leaders believe in the derivation of legitimacy from the public."*

> *"Abū Dharr al-Ghifārī, a companion of Muhammad, is credited by some scholars, like Muhammad Sharqawi and Sami Ayad Hanna, as a principal antecedent of Islamic socialism. He protested against the accumulation of wealth by the ruling class during Uthman's caliphate and*

*urged the equitable redistribution of wealth. The first Muslim Caliph Abu Bakr introduced a guaranteed minimum standard of income, granting each man, woman and child ten dirhams annually—this was later increased to twenty dirhams.*

*The first experimental Islamic commune was established during the Russian Revolution of 1917 as part of the Wäisi movement, an early supporter of the Soviet government. The Muslim Socialist Committee of Kazan was also active at this time.*

*In the modern era, Islamic socialism can be divided into two: a left-wing and a right-wing form. The left wing (Siad Barre, Haji Misbach, Ali Shariati, Yasser Arafat, Abdullah al-Alayli, and Jalal Al-e Ahmad) advocated proletarian internationalism, the implementation of Islamic Sharia, whilst encouraging Muslims to join or collaborate with international socialist or Marxist movements. Right-wing socialists (Mohammed Iqbal, Agus Salim, Jamal ad-Din Asad-Abadi, Musa al-Sadr, and Mahmud Shaltut) are ideologically closer to third positionism, supporting not just social justice, egalitarian society and universal equality, but also Islamic revivalism and implementation of Sharia. They also reject a full adoption of a class struggle and keep a distance from other socialist movements.*

*Revolutionary activity along the Soviet Union's southern border and Soviet decision makers recognized would draw the attention of capitalist powers and invite them to intervene. It was this understanding which prompted the Russian representation at the Baku Congress in September 1920 to reject the arguments of the national communists as impractical and counterproductive to the revolution in general, without elaborating their fear that the safety of Russia lay in the balance. It was this understanding, coupled with the Russian Bolsheviks' displeasure at seeing another revolutionary center proposed in their own domain revolutionary, that galvanized them into action against the national communists."*

If you are wondering why Christianity is targeted by the Communists and Islam gets a free pass with them, the foregoing passages ought to illustrate why this is. Extremist Islam is Marxist at its core and has been since the Bolshevik Revolution. The bloody 'justice' meted out by organizations such as ISIS falls right in line with the murderous tendencies of communists across the globe. History proves this. It should also be noted the similarity in dress between the black frocks worn by revolutionary Jesuits, Hitler's SS, ISIS and the modern Antifa movement. None of this is accidental. It is a symbolic representation of ideological solidarity in all these movements.

Within the realm of controlling consciousness, the use of symbols and symbolism plays a very important roll. While most of the public is blissfully ignorant of the meaning of symbols we find all around us in TV ads, movies, magazines, on billboards and elsewhere, symbols comprise a form of secret language within these subversive organizations through which they know the meaning of the symbols and the public at large does not. When organizations adopt any of these symbols in their organizational logos, they are communicating to their fellow travelers that their organization is part of the 'Great Work' as defined in Freemasonry, which is nothing more than the conquest of the planet hiding behind alleged religion and spirituality.

Although most of the public compartmentalizes the separate religions as being different and unconnected, there are intimate ties at the top leadership who are guiding their subordinates and their congregations down a road to Marxist global control. These seemingly divergent factions are all working for the same goal, and by keeping these things snugly compartmentalized in the public's mind, they are able to push their Globalist agenda ever closer to completion.

Once a religious doctrine is accepted, it creates a permanent blind spot in one's cognitive functions and their view remains tainted with the ideology and they do not generally see what has been revealed in this chapter. Once again, we have cognitive illusions displayed for what they are. Nothing is as it appears to our perceptions when we harbor such cognitive blind spots based on our respective faiths and are willing to defend them to the death. We become unwilling slaves supporting an agenda we know nothing about.

# 3. What is the Deep State?

While most Americans remain blissfully unaware of the reality that surrounds them as Western culture is under psychological assault, the term Deep State is still widely misunderstood. For some the Deep State only appears to be a corrupt gang of criminals who have permeated government bureaucratic offices at the highest level, including the FBI, DOJ, CIA and even into the U.S. Congress. A goodly percentage of Americans do not pay attention to the news broadcasts at all and don't even know the term Deep State. They live in a world of escapism and pay little to no attention whatsoever to what is going on in the political arena at all.

About 30% or more are attached to pushing leftist-leaning ideologies and, if we are lucky, maybe 50% are aware that something is terribly wrong in America but don't know how to identify what it is that's wrong aside from what limited news they are fed by a diminishing number of honest news broadcasters. For those who are keeping up with current events, they are aware of an intentional coup attempt to unseat a lawfully elected U.S. President perpetrated by the former administration of Barack Obama, which includes high-placed officials in the State Dept., the FBI, Department of Justice (DOJ), and CIA. Aside from these inside agency players, there have also been Globalist foreign intelligence agencies who have worked in collusion with these conspirators to reverse the will of the American voter by fabricating a false narrative that has gone on in the public arena for almost three years (the Mueller Investigation and House Democrat committee hearings), pushed hard by certain Democrats in power in Congress as well as their collaborators in the controlled left-wing media. This is a very real conspiracy and it is vast.

America, and virtually all Western governments, have been under psychological assault for well over a century through subversive actions as well as political posturing to lead the world down the road to total domination by the communist Globalists. It is, as yet, not widely reported just what the Deep State is, so I will do my utmost to clarify this issue for the reader and will also explain why the term Deep State is being used rather than the stark truthful statement about what it represents.

To get a better grasp on what is presently in full swing on U.S. soil, I highly recommend the reader to watch an hour-long video by a former KGB defector, Yuri Bezmenov, who reveals the communist plan for subverting nations. The video is entitled, *Yuri Bezmenov: Psychological Warfare Subversion & Control of Western Society (Complete).* I am providing links to the video on both Bitchute and YouTube.

https://www.bitchute.com/video/KvdknPVCt1kc/

The situation we are facing with the undermining of the American form of government has been a carefully orchestrated plan to secretly undermine the Constitution and the American way of life. This can also be said about the Western European nations, who themselves are awakening to how close the endgame of the Globalist communist conspiracy is to completion. There is no way I can explain all the permutations of this massive global conspiracy because it has been going on for centuries, if not millennia. I will be focusing more on the present situation with just enough background for the reader to perceive the overall picture, so they at least have some foundational knowledge of what is taking place.

We are about three generations removed from what is known as the McCarthy Era, or the time of the "Red Scare", when Senator Joseph McCarthy performed investigations into communist infiltration in the State Dept., U.S. Military and in Hollywood in the mid 1950's. McCarthy's name has been vilified over these investigations, yet history has proven that McCarthy was wholly correct in his concerns as well and what he discovered in his investigations. What has come to light since the fall of the Iron Curtain and access was gained to Russian records of the time, is that not only was McCarthy correct in his investigations, but the problem of communist infiltration was worse than even McCarthy surmised. Now that we are about 60 years or so past the McCarthy investigations, the infiltration by the communists into the Western world is even worse than when McCarthy did his Senate investigations. Although it has not yet been fully revealed to the American public at large, the enigmatic Deep State is nothing more than the Communist International hiding behind the mask of liberal Marxist Globalism.

If you watched the video by Yuri Bezmenov and how the KGB works to undermine a nation's trust in its law enforcement personnel, you will see this distrust at all levels, from the local police officials all the way up to complete distrust in the Federal law enforcement agencies based on the actions of James Comey and the other Obama administration conspirators. Everything that Bezmenov revealed in that video presentation has taken place and the Globalists are very close to toppling the American system of government if their plan isn't stopped. This is a fight to the finish in a winner take all game. Either communism will win, or President Trump and new allies in Europe and South America will bring the communist juggernaut to a complete loss.

Because mostly Jewish communists waged such a devastating propaganda campaign against Joe McCarthy and his alleged 'Witch Hunts' against a very real and present danger, bringing communism to the fore at the present time while reporting about the Deep State presents a very difficult hurdle where apprising the public is concerned. The commies are waiting in the wings to pull down President Trump using the same tactics they used to destroy Joe McCarthy, if he were to sound the alarm about creeping communism and its pervasive control in all aspects of American life at this time. I am providing a few short video presentations below about the Chinese communist incursion to the U.S. from *Epoch Times*. It is highly recommended that you take the time to watch these videos for your greater understanding, they are not that long.

*How Communism Subverted the Church*
https://www.youtube.com/watch?v=XegqiDFLZNI

*Chinese Subversion & Corruption of U.S.A is Deep and Far Reaching*
https://www.youtube.com/watch?v=O-Oah3DKbaA

*What's the Marxist Trojan Horse in the Democratic Party?*
https://www.youtube.com/watch?v=yHk6e9fpOU8

*EXPOSED: The Marxist Plot to Destroy Higher Education in America*
https://www.youtube.com/watch?v=PTFDoWxFZgA

*Why Socialism and Communism Are the Same*
https://www.youtube.com/watch?v=5IMecwZA3KA

If you watch any of the mainstream media, other than Fox news, you have been subjected to a form of mass brainwashing whereby the American public is being sold the lie that President Trump is a fascist, another Hitler. This is all communist propaganda and the major media outlets (Fox News not exempted with their own left-leaning reporters) are co-conspirators in the destruction of America by using subversive propaganda tactics to sow turmoil on our soil. Sadly, the younger generation who has fallen under communist brainwashing tactics in the educational system, has bought these lies and have become useful idiots to pushing the communist agenda inexorably forward. This is the basis of the conflict between the communist controlled Democrat party and the so-called religious right. Make no mistake, there are also Republicans who have sold out to the Globalist agenda. These Republicans are referred to as RINOs (Republican In Name Only) and they are as much a part of this cognitive subversive deception as the most rabid defenders of Socialism, seen with every current Democrat presidential candidate as well as the most vocal members of Congress who are pushing the Socialist agenda.

This is a psychological war and the last 60-70 years have been used to soften the American mind and put it to sleep through control of the media and the educational system to brainwash the public and our children. The Fabian communists have been exquisitely effective in waging this psychological warfare. This is the reality hiding behind the illusion of your everyday lives. The subversive communist element has been so well hidden and so well guarded over these decades that their invasion into every American institution has taken place without sounding the alarm for public awareness until very recently with the part of the public that is awakening from the media's hypnotic spell of propaganda.

It is the CIA who came up with the plan to destroy anyone looking into this real conspiracy by coining the term 'conspiracy theory'. With its collaborators in the media and a targeted campaign to fill the conspiracy arena with well-placed contrived false narratives to discredit anyone who saw through to the real conspiracy facts, the American public has been brainwashed into never looking at the true conspiracy. There are think tanks around the world whose sole occupation is to contrive wacky conspiracy narratives and peddle them to the public, things like the Flat Earth theory and government conspiracies hiding behind every bush, and through media brainwashing, the public's eyes glaze over when anyone tries to talk about these conspiracies. You must remember, the primary goal of the communists in any country they target for conquest, the people must lose all trust in their governments and police forces. Take a look around you and tell me what you see.

The more fanciful the conspiracy narrative that is spun out by these think tanks, the crazier the individual who falls for such contrived nonsense sounds when they try to explain it to others. Most have not seen through this designed program of conspiracy narrative propaganda brainwashing, and all too many fall prey to the ludicrous conspiracy lies peddled in the public arenas like YouTube, because believing the fantasy illusion is more exciting than digging out the hard, pragmatic truth. These wacky conspiracy theories are not challenged as much as they should be, but are instead allowed to proliferate in such public media platforms because it fits the agenda to not only confuse and confound the public, but also serves as a mask to hide the real conspiracy behind so no one listens to the truth if it is told to them.

With the over two-year Mueller investigation and the contrived Russiagate narrative spawned by the communists in this country, America is seeing the real conspiracy play out on the public stage. Sadly, because the CIA and other high-level government agencies have been co-opted by communist Globalist operatives, all too many people in the public bought into these fabricated conspiracy lies, thereby handicapping a presidency for pushing three years now. The communist propagandists in the media have worked tirelessly 24/7 since before the election of Donald Trump to undermine his presidency, ultimately seeking to destroy the American way of life. The discord you see in the public is by specific design and it has taken decades for the communist operatives to set the stage for this unrest. It is going to get worse before it gets better.

So, let's put things into some semblance of order here and illustrate what President Trump is up against in light of this ongoing communist subversion of America. The communists control virtually all the media in this country, and that includes social networking sites like Facebook, Twitter and especially Google. YouTube is owned by Google. The mainstream media (MSM) along with these social networking platforms are working for their communist masters in subverting the truth and censoring any voices that go against the communist leftist narrative. Evidence for all of this lies in the public arena, but mostly only through alternative independent media not owned by the tech and media giants. If you aren't specifically looking for this information, some of which is reported by a few diligent reporters on Fox news, you will hear nothing about it.

When we have an enemy ideological adversary operating with impunity on U.S. soil, how does this president take down the enemy when almost half the public believes the lies spun by the communist media? Any action he takes is going to be challenged as unamerican, which is why the Leftist media is pushing the lie about Trump being another Hitler to the public. The communists can only continue to hide their subversive actions by projecting their vile deeds onto a presidency which will eventually take down the communist agenda in America given the chance. The commies know this and that is why they are pushing back as hard as they are against anything this president does.

Because the commies did such a thorough job of tearing down Senator Joe McCarthy, if Trump were to challenge them outright as being communist subversive agents, the left-wing media would marshal their forces and tear him apart like they did Joe McCarthy. This explains why the term Deep State is being used at this time, but before all is said and done, the enemy on our soil will be exposed for what they truly are. It is because of the exquisite brainwashing and intentional dumbing-down of the American public over the last 70 years, and the false perception that communism died when the Berlin Wall came down, that few in the public can even perceive the true state of affairs on the global stage. The fact is that too many people in the public are not even paying attention to politics or anything else. They are willfully and blissfully ignorant of what has been explained in just the first few chapters of this book.

This war for America is already heating up with the release of communist subversive agents like Antifa creating mayhem in the streets. The communists have created their outposts in 'sanctuary cities' where they let the likes of Antifa perform their riotous acts without repercussions from sanctuary city law enforcement policies. The American system of jurisprudence has been steadily eroded over the years with communist sympathizer judges holding the majority vote on the U.S. Supreme Court for the last 70 years.

There are well-placed communist lawyers and judges at all levels of American legal system who have steadily pushed the communist agenda forward, hiding behind the mask of humanitarianism and women's rights and minority rights. By creating such minority enclaves, the communists have effectively fragmented America culture into warring camps. With the aid of the field of psychology, we now have gender-dysfunctional individuals being given minority rights for their psychological disorders, as but one example, which only further fragments our culture and pushes the communist agenda inexorably forward. If you wonder why all these things are happening, you have just been given an explanation why.

# 4. False Flags and Terrorism

To start this chapter, we must first define what a false flag is. Wikipedia gives us this information in part under *False Flag*:

*"A false flag is a covert operation designed to deceive; the deception creates the appearance of a particular party, group, or nation being responsible for some activity, disguising the actual source of responsibility.*

*The term "false flag" originally referred to pirate ships that flew flags of countries as a disguise to prevent their victims from fleeing or preparing for battle. Sometimes the flag would remain and the blame for the attack be laid incorrectly on another country. The term today extends beyond naval encounters to include countries that organize attacks on themselves and make the attacks appear to be by enemy nations or terrorists, thus giving the nation that was supposedly attacked a pretext for domestic repression and foreign military aggression.*

*Operations carried out during peacetime by civilian organizations, as well as covert government agencies, can (by extension) also be called false flag operations if they seek to hide the real organization behind an operation."*

With this brief set of definitions, you are now prepared to understand how subversive agents working within a targeted nation can fall prey to false flag operations. In every country that ever fell under the control of socialism the public had its arms removed from them so they could not protect themselves from the tyranny of communism if the need arose – which it always did. From the Bolshevik Revolution into Nazi Germany, disarming the public was a primary priority so the public could not defend itself from armed government forces. In the U.S. Constitution we have the 2nd Amendment to protect these citizen rights to keep and bear arms specifically for the purpose that if the government ever decided to wage war on its people, the people had the right and means to defend themselves.

The 2nd Amendment protection to keep and bear arms has been the primary target over the years to be removed by the communist invaders onto American soil. If you ever wondered why there is the continual push for gun control by the rabid communist Democrat party, it is because gun control *always* leads to gun confiscation in the end and leaves a populace unable to defend itself against tyranny.

In order to gain ground for gun control arguments by communist compromised legislators, we come face to face with the use of false flag operations designed to sway the uninformed public in favor of gun control measures by using terror tactics. While sanctuary cities like Chicago have mass shootings by Black on Black crimes that usually go unreported in the mainstream media, every time there is a White shooter, the communist media is all over such stories screaming them from the rooftops claiming White supremacy racist fabricated stories. Just on Labor Day weekend alone in Chicago there were 41 shootings and 7 deaths in Black on Black crimes, yet one White nutjob who had a history of mental disorders and who had just lost his job and shot up a bunch of people in Odessa, Texas, dominated the headlines all focused on him.

Racism is the latest card being played by the communist media and pushing the false narrative that these random shooters were all White supremacists doesn't hold water with thorough investigation. The Dayton shooter was obviously a Left-wing Antifa supporter, and the MSM did a hasty retreat on that story because the shooter didn't fit their subversive public narrative about White supremacists.

In order to convince the public of the need for gun control, the communists use *agents provocateurs* to do their dirty work for them. Some readers may be too young to remember the Kentucky Fried Chicken and McDonald's restaurant murders back in the 1980s. These restaurant attacks were all perpetrated and eventually led to the enactment of the Brady Bill, one of the first major control legislative acts. Since that time, we also had a bunch of school shooters who were snipers against school playgrounds which also supplied impetus to push forth more gun legislation. Most of these acts were perpetrated by subversive agents designed to create even more repressive gun control laws. Amazingly enough, after each of these rashes of shooting and the legislation was passed enacting further gun control, the shootings mysteriously stopped. How coincidental.

Today, with the communist agenda on the verge of finally being fully exposed to the American public, we have a plethora of false flag random shootings, again perpetrated in order to force more gun control laws, eventually designed to confiscate the weapons of lawful private gun owners. This is no different than what Hitler did in Germany, nor the communists in Russia, China and Venezuela.

Many of these 'random' shooters have a history of psychological problems and have come by their guns illegally. The gun control background checks do not keep criminals from circumventing the law to gain access to weapons. The Dayton shooter did not buy the guns he used himself but went through a second party to order the guns for him, which shows that background checks do little to curb illegal gun possession for one who knows how to circumvent the law.

Through legislation and court actions, the mentally disabled are no longer kept safely away from the public but are allowed to roam at will, since most mental institutions have been shut down in America. My personal take is that the closing of these institutions was contrived and allows the mentally ill to wander around in the public with no oversight whatsoever regarding their actions. Here again, the field of Psychology had some serious cards to play regarding closing these institutions for 'humanitarian' reasons. Unless one gets a court ordered confinement for the mentally deranged, these people cannot be held in hospitals and can sign themselves out within a few short hours of being taken into custody. The inmates truly run the asylum.

Within this framework, one never knows when a mentally ill individual might get their hands on a gun and go on a shooting spree. Couple with this the rampant invasion of illegal aliens who flock to the U.S. southern border from all parts of the world, and we don't know what type of criminal subversive elements might already be resident on our soil. The murderous MS13 gang is a global drug and human trafficking cartel and we have no shortage of these gang members operating within the U.S. This doesn't discount illegal Muslims who adhere to the tenets of ISIS who may just be biding their time, and untold violence is unleashed on a blissfully ignorant and terrorized public. This is how communist anarchists work to undermine nations form within. It has been their standard *modus operandi* for over a century.

Along with MS13 illegal aliens, we find the dregs from over 60 other countries also crossing the border illegally, many of them from countries with violent Muslim ideologies. At the present time, there are estimated 30 million illegal aliens in the U.S. and most of them are unmonitored and well hidden in the tapestry of our society. We can only wonder how many of these are sleeper agents for the communists who are only waiting for the right signal to sow chaos in the public arena through car bombings or other acts of terroristic destruction. Using the Merriam Webster definition, a sleeper cell is:

*"a terrorist cell whose members work under cover in an area until sent into action"*

With the influx of millions of illegals from all around the world, we don't know how many subversive agents are already on our soil just waiting for the right circumstances to come into play before they activate. With the ever-tightening noose around the necks of the Spygate perpetrators and the exposure of communist agents in the U.S. government, the chances that these sleeper agents will rise to the call as former President Obama, Hillary Clinton and high-level FBI, CIA, DOJ and other officials are indicted and arrested for the crime of treason should be of concern to every American. This is the most dangerous part of the Trump presidency, for when these treasonous perpetrators are brought to justice, then the backlash by communist subversives well embedded on our soil is very likely to happen. I am not seeking to sow panic, but awareness. We live in very dangerous times as we seek to uproot the communist poison from our soil and keep our way of life intact.

The greatest threat in all this is the total ignorance of most of the public where the communist invasion is concerned.

Through decades of media propaganda, the public has become inured to the lies and believes the illusion more than the truth presented in these pages. When this all comes out, and it will, the psychological shock to the public will be massive. When one adds the violence wrought by subversive agents operating on our soil to this cognitive chaos, we can only see a grim picture in the months and years ahead. To remedy this problem is not going to be an easy or pleasant task. There is going to be psychological pain to be faced as these truths are borne out once the public is finally informed of the truth in contradistinction to the illusionary lies they have been told about their reality.

If my assessment is correct, and we are confronted with wide-scale violence perpetrated by these sleeper cells, then the President will have little choice than to invoke martial law to protect the public safety. Naturally, if the communist media is still in control, then these necessary actions will once again draw false comparisons of the President to Hitler, seeking to garner public support to continue their communist agenda. As I stated, this is a psychological war driven by propaganda and controlling the mind of the public through intentional disinformation. If one does not have the correct information from which to draw an informed conclusion, then the propaganda machine may well hold sway over the public mind.

The communist tyrants have always feared an armed populace that can defend itself against tyranny, which is why we are seeing such a monumental push for gun control in America at this time. Every time a false flag shooter kills innocents for no reason only adds more fuel to the fire of the disarmament rhetoric. Any legislator that is pushing such legislative acts to subvert the 2nd Amendment is an enemy to America and should be viewed as communist operatives, whether they do so willingly, or through leveraged blackmail. This is not a political contest between Republicans and Democrats, it is a war between the American way of life against encroaching and well embedded communism. Don't let anyone fool you by masking their perfidy behind humanitarian rhetoric. The communists want the American public totally disarmed so they can finally fulfill their agenda for total global domination. America is the last domino to fall for this Globalist juggernaut. If you believe otherwise, then the fantasy world of illusion has your mind firmly in its clutches.

One thing is certain, the Antifa mobs and their useful idiot supporters on the left are growing larger and bolder and none of us knows what the signal might be that turns these mobs into seriously violent attackers on an innocent public and people's property. The cauldron of chaos is being stirred and the controlled left-wing media is not reporting these things to the public at large. This constitutes lies by omission and much of the public will be totally blindsided when violence does erupt, say perhaps when Hillary Clinton finally gets arrested for her own acts of treason.

The communist media talking heads are as complicit in this communist conspiracy as was the lapdog media in Germany under Goebbels and Pravda in Russia. These are not journalists, but communist operatives. The Antifa gangs are funded by George Soros, an avowed Marxist, as are any number of 501(c)3 and (c)4 tax free organizations worldwide. It is these tax-free organizations that I suggest will be discovered to be nothing but money laundering slush funds that lead straight to the pockets of crooked, lawyers, judges and politicians before all is said and done. Soros is the most prominent actor on this stage, but he is by far not the only one. Soros is just another communist Jew with deep pockets and fingers that reach into many of these 501(c) and (c)4 organizations. I am not being anti-Semitic for reporting this fact, but I am devoutly anti-communist.

Contrary to popular mythology, Hitler was not a Fascist. Hitler promoted National Socialism, which is where the word Nazi comes from. He was asked to join forces with Benito Mussolini when Mussolini's armies were being defeated by the British in North Africa. Because of this wartime alliance, the world has been sold the illusion that Hitler was a Fascist when he was in fact a socialist. Mussolini created the Fascist Party in Italy.

Claiming that Hitler was a Fascist is just another dog whistle false flag designed to keep the public from knowing about Hitler's brand of socialism so the communists can continue to peddle the socialist Utopian ideology to emotionally insecure victim classes presenting communist socialism as the defender of the downtrodden. In America today the communist revolutionaries come in all races and sexes. They started their counter-revolution, as they call it, by laying a foundation in the 1960s with groups like the Yippies and the Weathermen. For some excellent historical background on the Weathermen I highly recommend watching the hour-long video presented below. The video is only part one of what is expected to be a two-part documentary, but the information contained in the video should be required teaching in American school systems more than *Billy has Two Daddies* or *Heather has Two Mommies*.

*The WeatherMen - IPOT Presents - 6.21.19*
https://www.youtube.com/watch?v=9PjtV0RA8hE&t=14s

https://www.bitchute.com/video/HQWSdm4SGc4Z/

As you will note if you watch this video, violence and crime are part of the communist manifesto to sow terror in a target nation. The closer President Trump and those Americans who are aware of this communist threat get to prosecuting the major perpetrators of this psychological war against America and the world, the more you should expect to see random shooting incidents to play out on the public stage. In time, if it follows the communist anarchist patterns like those used in Russia leading up to the Bolshevik Revolution, we can expect bombings and other large-scale terrorist attacks before all is said and done. The fact is that it is not the guns perpetrating the mass shooting crimes, but communist operatives or mentally deranged individuals. How much of that have you heard on the news? Or have you only heard about White supremacists perpetrating these crimes by the controlled communist media? As things heat up in this war for America, always be aware of your surroundings. If you see something out of kilter, say something. Staying aware of your surroundings may be what it takes to ensure that you do not become a victim to such heinous communist crimes.

With the influx of illegals from around the world, we also will find ISIS operatives who take part in such public terror attacks. Perhaps now you may have a better understanding about why President Trump is working overtime to get that wall built at the southern border and why the communist Democrats are screaming bloody murder in seeking to stop its construction.

George Soros and other United Nations organizations, along with associated 501(c)3 and (c)4 organizations, working in collusion with communist Jesuit priests and nuns in Mexico and Central America, are funding this massive influx of illegals crossing our borders. The human trafficking aspect for the Mexican drug cartels is bringing them billions of dollars in smuggling fees and also sustains the market for pedophiles seeking young children for child sex trafficking. Communist China is producing the opium substitute fentanyl by the ton, which is one of the most dangerous drugs on the planet, and shipping it to the drug cartels to smuggle into the U.S. The U.S. is under assault from every direction possible, with enemies within and without, while half the population remains uninformed and uncaring. This is the world of reality that the fantasy world of illusion keeps away from the eyes of the public. Ignore it at your own peril.

# 5. The Coudenhove-Kalergi Plan

If you want to understand the illegal influx of third world migrants into the Western world, you have to go back to the beginning of the plan proposed by an Austrian Count named Richard von Coudenhove-Kalergi. While one must be careful with citations on Wikipedia, particularly with more modern history and the communist aim to control information, of which Wikipedia plays a great part as a 'go to' information source for many people, we can find some valid information about Kalergi from their posting under *Richard von Coudenhove-Kalergi:*

*"Richard Nikolaus Eijiro, Count of Coudenhove-Kalergi (16 November 1894 – 27 July 1972) was an Austrian-Japanese politician, philosopher and Count of Coudenhove-Kalergi. A pioneer of European integration, he served as the founding president of the Paneuropean Union for 49 years. His parents were Heinrich von Coudenhove-Kalergi, an Austro-Hungarian diplomat and Mitsuko Aoyama, the daughter of an oil merchant, antiques-dealer and major landowner in Tokyo. His childhood name in Japan*

*was Aoyama Eijiro. He became a Czechoslovak citizen in 1919 and then took French nationality from 1939 until his death.*

*His first book, Pan-Europa, was published in 1923 and contained a membership form for the Pan-Europa movement, which held its first Congress in 1926 in Vienna. In 1927, Aristide Briand was elected honorary president of the Pan-Europa movement. Public figures who attended Pan-Europa congresses included Albert Einstein, Thomas Mann and Sigmund Freud."*

*"Coudenhove-Kalergi's parents met when his mother helped the Austro-Hungarian diplomat after he fell off a horse while riding in Japan. In commenting on their union, Whittaker Chambers described the future originator of Pan-Europe as "practically a Pan-European organization himself." He elaborated: "The Coudenhoves were a wealthy Flemish family that fled to Austria during the French Revolution. The Kalergis were a wealthy Greek family from Crete. The line has been further crossed with Poles, Norwegians, Balts, French and Germans, but since the families were selective as well as cosmopolitan, the hybridization has been consistently successful."*

*The Kalergis family roots trace to Byzantine royalty via Venetian aristocracy, connecting with the Phokas imperial dynasty. In 1300, Coudenhove-Kalergi's ancestor Alexios Phokas-Kalergis signed the treaty that made Crete a dominion of Venice."*

*"Aristocratic in his origins and elitist in his ideas, Coudenhove-Kalergi identified and collaborated with such politicians as Engelbert Dollfuss, Kurt Schuschnigg, Otto von Habsburg, Winston Churchill, and Charles de Gaulle. His ideal political constituent was a gentleman who must respect and protect ladies, a person adhering to honesty, fair play, courtesy, and rational discourse. He strove to replace the nationalist German ideal of racial community with the goal of an ethnically heterogeneous European nation based on a commonality of culture[citation needed], a nation whose geniuses were the "great Europeans" such as abbé de Saint-Pierre, Kant, Napoleon, Giuseppe Mazzini, Victor Hugo, and Friedrich Nietzsche."*

*"Coudenhove-Kalergi is recognized as the founder of the first popular movement for a united Europe. His intellectual influences ranged from*

*Immanuel Kant, Rudolf Kjellén and Oswald Spengler to Arthur Schopenhauer and Friedrich Nietzsche. In politics, he was an enthusiastic supporter of "fourteen points" made by Woodrow Wilson on 8 January 1918 and pacifist initiatives of Kurt Hiller.* **In December 1921, he joined the Masonic lodge "Humanitas" in Vienna.** *In 1922, he co-founded [citation needed] the Pan-European Union (PEU) with Archduke Otto von Habsburg, as "the only way of guarding against an eventual world hegemony by Russia." In 1923, he published a manifesto entitled Pan-Europa, each copy containing a membership form which invited the reader to become a member of the Pan-Europa movement. He favored social democracy as an improvement on "the feudal aristocracy of the sword" but his ambition was to create a conservative society that superseded democracy with "the social aristocracy of the spirit."* **European freemason lodges supported his movement,** *including the lodge Humanitas. Pan-Europa was translated into the languages of European countries (excluding Italian, which edition was not published at that time) and a multitude of other languages, except for Russian."*

*"Hitler did not share the ideas of his Austrian compatriot. He argued in his 1928 Secret Book that they are unfit for the future defense of Europe against America. As America fills its North American lebensraum, "the natural activist urge that is peculiar to young nations will turn outward." But then "a pacifist-democratic Pan-European hodgepodge state" would not be able to oppose the United States, as it is "according to the conception of that commonplace bastard, Coudenhove-Kalergi..." Nazi criticism and propaganda against Coudenhove-Kalergi, and his European worldview, would decades later form the basis of the racist Kalergi plan conspiracy theory.*

**Nazis considered the Pan-European Union to be under the control of Freemasonry.** *In 1938, a Nazi propaganda book Die Freimaurerei: Weltanschauung, Organisation und Politik was released in German.* **It revealed Coudenhove-Kalergi's membership of Freemasonry, the organization suppressed by Nazis.** *On the other hand, his name was not to be found in Masonic directories 10,000 Famous Freemasons published in 1957–1960 by the United States' freemasons. He had already left the Viennese Masonic Lodge in 1926 to avoid the criticism that had occurred at* *that time against the relationship between the Pan-European movement and Freemasonry. He wrote about his Masonic membership in Ein Leben für Europa (A Life for Europe) published in 1966. In fact, its Nazi propaganda book also described his action in 1924–1925 only. However, this propaganda also stated that "The Grand Lodge of Wien went enthusiastically to work for the Pan European Union in a call to all Masonic chief authorities. Even **the Masonic newspaper** The Beacon enthused about the thoughts of the higher degree Freemason Coudenhove-Kalergi, and stated in March 1925: "Freemasonry, especially Austrian Freemasonry, may be eminently satisfied to have Coudenhove-Kalergi among its members. Austrian Freemasonry can rightly report that Brother Coudenhove-Kalergi fights for his Pan European beliefs: political honesty, social insight, the struggle against lies, striving for the recognition and cooperation of all those of good will. In this higher sense, Brother Coudenhove-Kalergi's program is a Masonic work of the highest order, and to be able to work on it together is a lofty task for all brother Masons.""*

[Bold emphasis mine]

To illustrate the disinformation in the passages cited at Wikipedia above about the. . . .

*"Nazi criticism and propaganda against Coudenhove-Kalergi, and his European worldview, would decades later form the basis of the racist Kalergi plan conspiracy theory."*

We only need to look at the words of Coudenhove -Kalergi himself in *Practical Idealism*, where he plainly states on pages 21-22:

*"Inbreeding strengthens the character, weakens the mind – crossing weakens the character and strengthens the Spirit. Where inbreeding and crossbreeding meet under happy auspices, they witness the highest type of human being the strongest character connects with the sharpest mind. Where in unfortunate auspices of inbreeding and mix meet, they create degeneration types with a weak character, dull mind.* **The man of the distant future will be hybrid. Today's races and the boxes are increasing the overcoming of space, time and Prejudice fall victim. The Eurasian-Negroid Future race, externally similar to the ancient Egyptian, the diversity of peoples with a will Replace diversity of personalities.** *For, according to the laws of inheritance increases with the Diversity of the ancestral diversity, the uniformity of the ancestors Uniformity of the offspring."*

I cite these passages to illustrate how information has been intentionally altered from the truth in these Wikipedia passages when compared with the words of Count Coudenhove-Kalergi. One must always be wary of information offered on Wikipedia about personalities over the last century or so since the creation of the British Fabian Society. Wikipedia is more reliable when it comes to ancient history than with modern history.

Having read all that, let's cut to the chase and face reality. Kalergi's idea of a Pan Europe has become the modern EU. This is indisputable fact. Kalergi's plan to reduce the masses of humanity into a Eurasian-Negroid racial hodge-podge of a single race is stated plainly as just proven. Contrary to some Wikipedia sources, Kalergi was a Leftist elitist who collaborated with the international bankers harboring the dream of ultimately having a Jewish ruling class over the coffee-colored masses of the human race.

If you want to understand the influx of illegal migrants from the poorest countries of the world into Europe and America, we only need look to the Coudenhove-Kalergi Plan to understand what is taking place. Whether it is through rape or willful miscegenation, the elimination of the White race by mixing it with other races to create the Kalergi polyglot race of the Marxist future is well in progress. At least, this is what assaulted Europeans bemoan about the illegal invasion of refugees into Europe. What these fearful White people fail to realize in their own paranoia and fear is what Coudenhove-Kalergi actually sought, and that was the total extinction of *all* racial differences, not just the Whites. If his plan were to succeed, every race on the planet would disappear into Coudenhove- Kalergi's homogenized Eurasian-Negroid race, except the Jews, who Kalergi thought were the most 'spiritual' Master Race on the planet (See pages 48-51 of *Practical Idealism* at the .pdf file link below). He reached this conclusion even after the Bolshevik Revolution and its murderous policies.

I read a science fiction novel many years ago called *This Perfect Day* written by the author of *Rosemary's Baby*, Ira Levin. Within that novel this blending of the races into a single homogenous whole had already been fulfilled. There was never any explanation on how or why this came about, it was just a given tenet of the novel. Within this world of wonderful coffee-colored slant-eyed human population, the culture was kept under the influence of drugs and every family had their own psychologist advisor. While Orwell's *1984* and Aldous Huxley's *Brave New World* have held center stage as two distinct types of a dystopian future, Levin's novel has slipped through the cracks and has not gotten the same notoriety with the public.

In Levin's version of this dystopian future, the world is governed by a secret elite (mirrored by our present reality) whose ultimate game is control of the masses to suit their personal agenda for global domination. The three novels just listed are not warnings but are in fact representative of at least three different plans being presently executed by the globalist communist elite. We have Orwell's Big Brother *1984* surveillance society being built all around us; we have the abuse of psychologists dispensing mind numbing drugs to their emotionally challenged patients coming close to Huxley's *Brave New World*, and the forced miscegenation of races according to the Coudenhove-Kalergi plan with illegal immigration that will ultimately lead to Levin's dystopian future from *This Perfect Day*. Combine these three scenarios together and you see the world the Fabian Society communist social engineers are designing for humanity - if it isn't stopped in its tracks.

Those who have sought to expose the Coudenhove-Kalergi plan are called racists and White supremacists because they do not believe in the rape and destruction of American and European cultures. I am providing a link below for short 8-minute video entitled, *Coudenhove-Kalergi plan for white genocide explained...* to add a bit more information on all this. The Globalists don't want this information available to the public and the video has been banned on YouTube as 'hate speech'. Communist censorship is becoming rampant in Western alternative media at the hands of companies like Google, who owns YouTube. If the link below fails to work (which it did at the time I wrote this book), then the censors have removed it from the internet.

https://archive.org/details/CoudenhoveKalergiPlanForWhiteGenocideExplained...

I am posting a link below for an English translation of Coudenhove-Kalergi's book, *Practical Idealism* in .pdf format if you want to read the words of the man responsible for this immigration crisis in Europe and America in his own words.

https://archive.org/details/PracticalIdealism-EnglishTranslation

The purpose of this book is to educate and inform my readers about the ugly truth hiding behind all the communist claims of the illegal migration crisis being a 'humanitarian crisis'. It is a formulated plan for devious social engineering, and humanitarianism is only the deceptive mask it hides behind to advance this secretive assassination of all races and blend humanity into one controllable race. Humanitarianism is the fantasy world that hides the ugly truth of the reality just revealed. One can either fall for the propaganda or they can pull the blinders off and face reality head on.

On a personal note, I have no emotional stake in who decides to marry who racially or otherwise. Human history has shown that rape and incest have haunted humanity since before the written word was handed down to humanity by its gods and priests. I find it highly doubtful that there is any such thing as a 'pure' race anywhere on this planet. If humanity decides on its own through the course of its evolution that these presumed racial traits should all be merged into a single planetary race, then let evolution decide the matter. My personal problem with the Coudenhove-Kalergi plan is the deliberate and tyrannical form of forced social engineering it has historically shown itself to be. No tyrant or group of self-appointed tyrants should wield that kind of authority, and it should bother you as much as the tyranny is detestable to me.

With the supporting information in the video links in this chapter, the reader now has a firm foundation for further investigation into this matter. Don't take my word for any of this, read Coudenhove-Kalergi's own words on the matter. Dig, and do your own research and stop being a slave to the fantasy world of false compassion and humanitarianism which is only designed to keep you enslaved to the fantasy world and keep reality hidden from you.

# 6. The Trusts

One of the continuing lies in the fantasy world is the presumed conflict between Capitalism and Communism. At one time this may have been true, but at the present it is as far removed from reality as one can get.

The very first Trust ever created was in 1882 by John D. Rockefeller with the Standard Oil Company. For some background on these trusts I direct the reader to a synopsized version about *Monopolies and Trusts* at Encyclopedia.com. The link is provided below:

http://globaltable.org.uk/wp/wp-content/uploads/2016/02/RUNNYMEDE_GAZETTE_1602.pdf

What should be noted after reading relevant segments of the article, which I am precluded from sharing directly due to copyright laws, is that President Theodore Roosevelt was one of the first *Progressive* Presidents. For clarification's sake, Progressive in the late 1800s to early 1900s still meant socialist.

After Rockefeller created his trust to consolidate and monopolize the oil business, other monopolistic 'Robber Barons' soon followed suit in the railroad industry and the steel industry with the Carnegie Foundation. These trusts (foundations) have changed their outer garments today and operate, at least publicly, as non-profit organizations allowed to operate under the 501(c)3 and (c) 4 tax laws. They present themselves as philanthropic organizations, but they use their funding primarily to underwrite the Globalist political agenda. Their 'benevolent' donations are most often contributions to left-leaning causes.

Probably the largest charitable Trust on the planet is the Lucis Trust created by Alice and Foster Bailey which initially served as a publishing company called Lucifer Publishing to print and promote Alice Bailey's work for the Theosophical Society. Due to the protest of the word Lucifer in the publishing company's name, it was eventually altered to Lucis Trust. Lucis Trust currently oversees almost 31,000 subdivisions worldwide, all organized as tax-free charitable trusts. The United Nations is a charitable trust that falls under the Lucis Trust umbrella.

Hiding behind the mask of selling a mystical form of spirituality, the Theosophical Society, working in collusion with the Lucis Trust, is the springboard for the modern New Age and other varied spiritual movements. The Theosophical Society, as mentioned in previous chapters, is intimately associated with the Marxist Fabian Society and the Society for Psychical Research. They also work closely with Masonic Lodges around the planet to advance the 'Great Work' moving toward total global domination.

For more information for the Great Work, or Great Work of the Ages I provide the links below – *The Great Work in*

*Speculative Freemasonry*, and a Wikipedia link for *The Great Work (Hermeticism)*:

http://www.masonicworld.com/education/articles/THE-GREAT-WORK-IN-SPECULATIVE-FREEMASONRY.htm

https://en.wikipedia.org/wiki/Great_Work_(Hermeticism)

Count Coudenhove-Kalergi was closely associated with the Rothschild global banking interests, as are the Rockefeller Foundation, the Carnegie Foundation and numerous other charitable trusts. The leadership in the Theosophical Society, Alice Bailey and Annie Besant were both members of the Fabian Society, with Annie Besant being a self-professed communist before becoming a co-founder of the British Fabian Society. While Madame Helena Blavatsky headed up the American branch of the Theosophical Society, Annie Besant took over management of the Eastern branch which was set up in India. Besant and the Theosophical Society played a key role in the Indian Independence Movement, which if one studies deeply enough past the illusionary sanitized superficial history of the Movement, was a Fabian Society cum Theosophical Society plan. Diligent research will show how the great Indian peacemaker was a pedophile and Theosophist.

Although Alice Bailey never held the position of president over the American branch of the Theosophical Society, she played a key influential role in directing the Society and its millions of members worldwide through her writings.

Through being classified as charitable trusts, all these organizations can take in billions of tax-free dollars and use these trusts as instruments for laundering money through to other communist front organizations, also masquerading as charitable organizations. There are millions of 501(c)3 and (c)4 organizations in the United States alone that go basically unmonitored by the IRS because it simply doesn't have the manpower to police them all. Due to this behemoth workload, there is no one watching these charitable foundations to monitor if they are playing by the rules or not.

In 1901 George Bernard Shaw, one of the founding members of the British Fabian Society published a pamphlet called *Socialism for Millionaires*. The link below will take you to a .pdf copy of this document. With this one document you will learn where the 'spare' millions of millionaires and charitable trusts go in truth.

http://collections.mun.ca/PDFs/radical/SocialismForMilli onaires.pdf

New York Jewish bankers like Jacob Schiff and Kuhn, Loeb and Assoc. underwrote financing for the Bolshevik Revolution. Without funding from rich Capitalists, the Socialist experiment in Russia would have utterly failed. The lie that is fed the public about the communists warring against the capitalists is contrived perceptual illusion and nowhere near the truth. A lie to make the public choose sides in a non-existent war. The multi-national corporations have been snugly in bed with the communist socialists for over a century. Without capitalist money to support the communist regimes, they would all fail. This is what President Trump is doing in this trade war with communist China and the European Union – seeking to cut off American purse strings for communist socialist enterprises. He is cutting access to the U.S. taxpayer piggy bank which has supported Marxist communism for over a century.

The United States was hoodwinked into fighting two world wars on behalf of Europe and we have paid to rebuild Europe twice after each of those wars. Without U.S. funding, half of Europe would probably still be in ruin because socialism can only survive on other-people's money. When I see cretins like the French President Macron and the Socialist Angela Merkel refuse to pay their fair share of NATO obligations, my own personal thought is that the U.S. ought to pull military aid and our troops out of these ingrate Marxist countries. The same applies to the entire EU.

The war against capitalism is a lie in our modern era. The richest Capitalists are already in bed with the Marxist Globalists and subjugating all of humanity is the sole thing they are interested in. So long as people embrace this illusion about the war between capitalism and communism, you are living in a fantasy world. You are buying the illusion and not seeing reality. I can only imagine how hard the Wall Street bankers laughed at the protests by the leftist Anonymous organizations in their Occupy Wall Street movement. That was all a contrived smoke and mirrors display for left-leaning useful idiots who do not have a clue about the game being played.

While Antifa and the leftist brainwashed college students protest about the multi-national corporations and their Capitalist ideology, they are utterly clueless to the fact that these same multi-national corporations are underwriting and paying for their protests through the 501(c) 3 and (c)4 organizations that cover the cost of their organizers, their poster supplies and T-shirts. Talk about irony! If these multi-national corporations and organizations like the Rockefeller and Carnegie Foundations were to stop the money influx into the Fabian Marxist agenda, these radical useful idiots couldn't organize a Sunday Social. If not for these corporate sponsors running ads in the newspapers or through social networking to pay protesting attendees, they would not be able to gather the stupid and uninformed clowns that attend these rallies. But, hey, that's life living in the illusion, so what else can be expected?

Imagine my amazement when the day after I composed this chapter that this news article showed up on Fox News by former Congressman Jason Chaffetz. Do you need any more verification about my assertions on the abuse of the 501(c)3 and (c)4 charitable trusts? The article is entitled, *Jason Chaffetz: Activists are weaponizing charitable giving -- And that means big trouble for every American.*

https://www.foxnews.com/opinion/jason-chaffetz-weaponizing-charitable-giving

For those who doubt the reach and influence of the Fabian Society, I am posting a link below for a .pdf file to a book entitled *Fabian Freeway: High Road to Socialism in the U.S.A.* published in 1966 by Rose L. Martin. Get informed about the truth and step out of the illusion. There is a wealth of evidence on the internet about the Fabian Society if one can break the spell of cognitive laziness of living in the illusion to free themselves from the mind control and find the reality of truth that hides behind these illusions.

https://mises.org/sites/default/files/Fabian%20Freeway%20High%20Road%20to%20Socialism%20in%20the%20USA%20-Digital%20Book_3.pdf

In the age of the Robber Barons, there were no child labor laws and there were no 40-hour work weeks. People had to work as long as their corporate masters dictated. There was no compensation for injuries or death on the job. The worker was simply replaced with another one and the injured party was left to fend for themselves after the fact. There were no workplace safety regulations and many workers in their varied trades did their jobs in often hazardous conditions on a daily basis. It was in this environment that Marxist Socialism found fertile ground to organize strikes and eventually start the trade unions. The

Marxists thought that if they could get the workers of the world to unite, they could destroy this type of Robber Baron capitalism and monopolistic practices.

This is the foundation of the class struggle, as Marxists call it. It was first seen before Marx wrote his *Communist Manifesto* in the French Revolution. The revolution wasn't against capitalism, per se, but stood against the tyranny of the aristocracy designed to unseat sitting monarchs and replace them with oligarchic democracy. Although the lower classes were used as the cannon fodder in the French Revolution, their lot in life didn't change much with the rise of the Masonic-created Reign of Terror that followed the Revolution. While communist ideologies profess elevating the position of the working man to get them to rise up and fulfill their own elitist agenda, the people never gain an inch after the fact, ever remaining subject to the whims of the replacement elite. Sadly, with the short human lifespan, it only takes about three generations for humans to forget these things and the pattern just keeps repeating itself.

This short overview provides a working basis for understanding who the Marxists target when they spark their revolutions, and who comes out the biggest losers, i.e. the common man they lie about wanting to protect. It's time the world wakes up and smells the coffee and shakes itself free of these illusions and steps into pragmatically and boldly facing reality. To do otherwise will only leave you in chains, slaves to fabricated perceptual illusions fostered by those who only want to rule your mind and your every move.

# 7. The Freemasons

This chapter is not going to be an exhaustive deep dive into Freemasonry and its role in this scheme for global domination. My intent is to provide enough information for the reader to use as a springboard to delve more deeply into this subject and all the others presented in this volume. I can't free your mind from the illusion, only you can. I am only pointing out the doorway out of the illusion. It is up to the reader to decide whether to step through that doorway to cognitive freedom or not.

Freemasonry claims an ancient legacy regarding its mythical origins. The Craft, as it refers to itself, is rife with ancient Egyptian, Greek and Jewish symbolism, much of which I have explained in my prior works, *Gutting Mysticism,* and more extensively in The *Truth About the 'Divine' Soul.* Although Freemasons must profess a belief in a Divine power in one form or another to join the Order, it is an occult religion driven by a Platonic agenda to create a world State put forth by Plato in *The Republic.*

I am going to provide some quotes from an unlikely source, a work entitled *Freemasonry: Ideology Organization and Policy* written by a Nazi named Dieter Schwarz. By providing this historical background should by no means be construed that I endorse Nazi Socialist policies or ideologies. What the reader must realize is that we often have to look to the detractors of an ideology to get closer to the truth about such organizations. Some of the best research into Freemasonry and the occult has been done by Christian researchers on the subject. The reader is advised to remember that this was a report written for the Nazi party and will have that political spin found in places, so the reader must read past the Nazi ideology to glean the meat from the text.

This book opens with these three paragraphs:

*"Freemasonry is an ideological form of hostility to National Socialism, the significance of which, in the development of the past two centuries must be deemed comparable to the effects of other supranational organizations, the political churches, world Jewry, and Marxism. In its present form, it must be viewed as the bourgeois-liberal advance troops of World Jewry.*

*It corrupts the principles of all forms of government based on racial and folkish considerations, enables the Jews to achieve social and political equality and paves the way for Jewish radicalism through its support for the principles of freedom, equality, and brotherhood, the solidarity of peoples, the League of Nations and pacifism, and the rejection of all racial differences.*

*With the help of its international connections and entanglements, Freemasonry interferes in the foreign policy relationships of all peoples, and pursues, through governmental leaders, secret foreign and world policies which escape the control of those in government."*

[Bold emphasis mine]

Now we must scrape away the Nazi residue about its racial policies and read through to what is being revealed. Barring its opposition to National Socialism, or vice versa, everything reported in the above three paragraphs regarding Freemasonry is wholly accurate. The next paragraph in this book hits the nail on the head:

*"Through its personal influences and economic favoritism, Freemasonry ensures that all dominant positions of the public, economic, and cultural life of a people are filled with lodge brethren, who in fact translate the concepts of Freemasonry into action."*

With these few paragraphs we have a synopsized and honest analysis of Freemasonry. Any study of history will prove that many heads of state, leaders in finance and education have been Freemasons. The lower degrees, what they call the Blue Degrees are generally rank and file businessmen who adhere to the lodges for the financial benefits the organization can offer to their business endeavors. The Masons take care of their own. The Blue Degree members are usually clueless about the criminal activities and the overall Socialist agenda held in secret by the higher-level members in the 33$^{rd}$ degree category and above. Make no mistake, there are close to 100 degrees of status within Freemasonry. As Albert Pike, the Confederate general and creator of Scottish Rite Freemasonry admitted in *Morals and Dogma*, "The Blue Degrees are only the outer portico", meaning that the first three degrees are there for public appearance only, and these Blue Degree lackeys provide the 'benevolent' front that masks the true intent of the nastier higher degrees. As Pike further admitted in *Morals and Dogma*, "The Adepts are the Princes of Freemasonry." It should be noted that there is no statue of any other Confederate General in Washington, D.C., yet to this day a statue of Albert Pike, the Grand Wizard and creator of Scottish Rite Freemasonry stands in Judiciary Square.

Masonry hides behind the idea of stone masons representing a form of their tradecraft. For public consumption, 'the Craft' is believed to represent this tradecraft but, in actuality, the Craft refers to a form of mystical witchcraft, which I explained thoroughly in *The Truth About the 'Divine' Soul*. Schwarz's book is only 70 pages long and can be found in .pdf format at the link below for those interested in a deeper dive into the matter of Freemasonry. Other volumes from Christian sources will be found as this chapter continues.

Where the public gets deceived in all these Globalist shenanigans is where we find the pot painting the kettle black. We see these political organizations excoriating their sister organizations, banning them, members quitting and things of this nature, all to serve as a blind to the fact that despite criticism and banning, this is all for public consumption. All of this is purely optics to support the perceptual world of illusion. This is exemplified with George Orwell and H.G. Wells, who were both members of the British Fabian Society, and quit the Society but still kept their revolutionary attitudes. Such acts are designed to confuse the public and never allow the public to see through this type of deceptive chicanery. It is all a form of psychological manipulation. As I stated previously, in the fantasy world of perceptual illusion, nothing is as it appears. How a situation looks through 'optics' isn't necessarily the true picture.

The Freemasons are occultists and openly worship Lucifer. Where Christian researchers fail in their conclusions is in the belief that the Lucifer referred to in Masonic lore is a male Angel who warred against the Jewish God and was cast out of heaven. That legend is a total fallacy, but it serves to blind the public of who the Masonic Lucifer really represents.

Lucifer is referred to as the Morning Star. The Morning Star is the planet Venus. Venus was the Roman goddess who was equated with the Greek goddess Aphrodite. The Masons worship the ancient Mother Goddess in all her varied guises over the ages. Since the Romantic philosophers came on the scene after the Enlightenment philosophers, the world has seen a resurgence of worshipping the alleged 'Divine Feminine'. *Lucifer is a goddess, not a fallen angel.* I discussed this at length in my book, *We Are Not Alone – Part 3: The Luciferian Agenda of the Mother Goddess.*

The Freemasons are intimately tied in with the Theosophical Society and both organizations often use the same symbolism. We will find the triangle and the Eye of Horus used in both ideologies. As noted earlier, the Theosophical Society is a sister organization to both the Fabian Society and the SPR. These three organizations form a triangle engaged in fostering the Globalist agenda, with the SPR representing the mind (psychology), the Fabian Society representing the body (politic) and the Theosophical Society representing the spirit (religious homogenization). When you understand this triumvirate of Globalist power then you understand all the talk about body, mind and spirit that permeates the marketplace today.

Through collaborating with the giant Trusts and charitable foundations worldwide, along with the international network of Masonic lodges, this power triumvirate has created a networking stranglehold on every avenue of human pursuits. The only way it can be defeated is to brings all its secrets to light, which I have personally sought to do with all my works. The illusion must be destroyed in order for the truth of reality to wake the slumbering and ignorant public from the illusion.

Through continual and massive efforts of psychological manipulation and propaganda, the public in general refuses to see the reality of these things, particularly when they are tirelessly fed information about lunatic 'conspiracy theories.' This type of psychological manipulation has made the public uninquisitive and totally accepting of the lie. When you add in the element of purposely distorted and fictitious conspiracy nonsense fed by Fabian and Theosophical Society operatives into public arenas like YouTube and elsewhere, it is easy to make people turn off their minds when the word conspiracy is uttered.

It takes some diligent research to discover that some of the worst purveyors of fake conspiracy theories over the past 2-3 decades are intimately associated with the alleged Truth Movement and the Theosophical Society and, unfortunately, many adherents to the Truth Movement conspiracy network haven't developed the discernment to see through the conspiracy theory deception. Many have become gullible and unwitting agents of the Globalist agenda by spreading these false conspiracy lies. This is one reason the public generally considers conspiracy theories to be nonsense. Sadly, most of what is in the public arena is an admixture of some historical truths and lots of contrived conspiracy nonsense.

This is psychological programming at its best. It reinforces the illusional reality and keeps people from dealing with the reality that lies beyond the illusion. This cognitive illusion could be equated with *The Matrix*. This rabbit hole of deception goes much deeper than will be presented in this volume, but I have covered it extensively in my other work, and there is no shortage of information that reveals much of this cognitive scam by other researchers over the last century. A good starting place can be found in the following books:

*Occult Theocrasy by Lady Queensborough*
https://www.globalgreyebooks.com/occult-theocrasy-ebook.html

*Light-bearers of Darkness*
https://archive.org/details/OccultTheocracyLadyQueenboroughA.k.a.Edith

*Trail of the Serpent*
https://archive.org/details/trailserpentano00bradgoog/page/n5

These volumes will reveal the occult nature of the Luciferian Freemasons, although the authors have fallen for the male Lucifer angel mythology and didn't see the goddess-worshiping nature of the Craft. If one reads my book, *The Truth About the 'Divine' Soul*, they will have in their hands the key to unraveling all these Masonic mysteries. I don't say this to peddle my book, but I spent almost 500 pages explaining the background and nature for all these mysteries which are more than can be contained in this volume.

Freemasonry is based on Plato's ideology of the State, which he professed ought to be controlled by 'enlightened philosophers.' Marxism is also founded on this Platonic principle. Where Hitler wanted to create a Socialist nation state, the Fabian Marxists want to create an international Globalist State, erasing all national boundaries to create their one world government, or New World Order. Through the writings of Orwell, Huxley and Levin, we see this world taking shape before our very eyes, if we can but remove the blinders of the illusion that keep our minds captive and merely putty in the hands of the psychological controllers.

Karl Marx's father was a rabbi. Much of Marxism finds its foundations in Jewish occult teachings in the Cabala. Masonry is also steeped in mystical Cabalistic practices in its magical workings. As much as the reader may scoff at the idea of magic, I explained its working principles in *The Truth About the 'Divine' Soul*, providing no shortage of evidence to support my assertions in that volume. Real 'magic', and I use that term very loosely given the nature of how Hollywood and sensationalist fiction promotes it to the public, has a very sound explanation, albeit a very troubling one to face. It is nothing like the illusion peddled to the public mind.

Masonry finds it foundations in the Renaissance period with the rediscovery of the Neoplatonist texts allegedly attributed to the writings of the ancient sage, Hermes Trismegistus. All Masonic occult traditions arise from these writings which sparked the Renaissance era. From these writings we later find the formation of the Rosicrucian secret society, whose members laid the foundation for modern academia through the Royal Society. It is from these roots that Freemasonry finds its heritage. Regardless of the claim of ancient lineage tracing back to Egyptian stone masons and the builders of Solomon's Temple, Masonry rides on the back of Plato and Neoplatonist texts reintroduced to the West at the time of the Renaissance. These so-called Hermetic texts include some early remnants of Gnostic teachings, of which a library of texts was found in 1945 in Nag Hammadi, Egypt called the *Nag Hammadi Library*.

As the quoted passages in the first part of this chapter assert, Freemasonry is well steeped in Jewish mysticism and Cabalistic teachings. Of this there can be no denial. For those interested in an in-depth website devoted to exposing Freemasonry and its many high-powered political members, the link below for Freemasonry Watch is provided for deeper research opportunities. This is not conspiracy 'theory', but conspiracy fact. Although some of the data presented on this website may be questionable in some cases, the researcher is cautioned to read with discernment and always check alternative sources for verification.

https://freemasonrywatch.org/

The fact is that no one will see through the illusion to find the truth of reality without doing their own research, and by research I don't mean simple cursory examinations of information then forming half-baked opinions based on little in-depth research. This is one of the major failings of people caught in the conspiracy disinformation network. All too many people read one article or see a short video on YouTube and form their opinions without the required research to actually know what is going on. It is due to this type of cognitive laziness and the desire to believe that one knows what they are talking about that makes conspiracy facts get lost behind uninformed conspiracy opinions.

Unearthing the truth is hard. There is no free pass to moving past the illusion into reality. Laziness in this process will not serve anyone in the pursuit of real truth. It takes time and dedication to get to the bottom of all this, and one will not get the full picture from perusing soundbite presentations on YouTube and elsewhere. This conspiracy has been going on for millennia, and anyone who thinks viewing a 10-30-minute video will provide them the answers they seek is gravely misinformed. Do the work and you will be amazed at what you can discover.

# 8. The Illusion of 'We the People'

*"Those who own the country ought to govern it." – John Jay, slogan of the Federalist Party*

As much as the title of this chapter may rankle many Americans, the belief in 'We the People' controlling our government is an utter sham. America is a divided nation and always has been. With the incursion of creeping Fabian Globalist communism, we are more fragmented as a people now than we ever were. The fact of the matter is that the Federal government for the most part is a government of, by and for lawyers and lobbyists. The House of Representatives was designed to be the people's House, and at one time it was to a degree. Presently, the people's House is ruled by lawyers and demagogues. It does not reflect the true will of the people and virtually everyone serving in the government on local, State and Federal levels has been compromised in one form or another. The issues the people think is their 'will', is dictated to them by the Mockingbird media. The issues dictated by the media become the public will, whether people want to admit this dismal fact or not.

Many people holding high positions in the three branches of Federal government are activist communist usurpers or have been blackmailed by foreign powers like Israel to keep feeding them foreign aid to the neglect of American citizens. Despite the illusion posited by the Declaration of Independence, 'We the People' started out as a government by and for the propertied and monied classes. This is an absolute fact of history. When the Constitution was framed, the common man, often illiterate, was never considered to have a participatory voice in the Federal government. It was only through stages that the common people came to have the right to vote. Again, this is historically verifiable fact, as unpleasant as this truth may be to bear.

America was colonized by mostly Protestant religious people. They had already broken with the Papacy during the Protestant Revolution, and the last thing they wanted on the soil of this nation was a bunch of Catholics governed by a foreign potentate – the Pope. What these Protestants didn't know was that the Church of Rome owned all the land in the Western hemisphere based on the Papal Bull of 1493, whereby Pope Alexander VI made this uncontested claim after Columbus purportedly 'discovered' the Americas.

For those who doubt the importance of the *Papal Bull Inter Caetera* May 4, 1493, we must ask why it is the second document in Commager's *Documents of American History*. I am providing a link below so you can read the Papal Bull for yourself.

*Papal Bull Inter Caetera*
http://www.uintahbasintah.org/usdocuments/doc4.pdf

What follows in this chapter is going to be upsetting to most Americans, but it is the truth, nonetheless. As revealed in the *Papal Bull Inter Caetera*, the Vatican Pope, by his own claim of authority as the pontiff on St. Peter's throne, claimed all land in the Western hemisphere. You can rest assured that every place a Catholic institution was set up anywhere on the planet, that an equal unsubstantiated claim of the land in any region representatives of the Church set foot, resulted in a similar claim of land by pure fiat of the power the Papacy, which it felt it singularly possessed as God's representatives on Earth. From the standpoint of the Papacy, the Roman Church owns the world. Although this Papal land theft has no bearing in contract law because it is a one-sided contract – an adhesion contract, until the power of the Vatican is challenged and taken down, this legal chicanery still stands as law. Two billion Catholics won't stand still for the destruction of their religious institution nor their Pope. This is quite a protective coercive mechanism to not mess with the status quo.

When the thirteen original colonies broke away from England, you can rest assured that Vatican representatives soon informed their leadership about who owned the land upon which they intended to build their nation. The fact is that the King's Charters which covered the land grants in the New World, were already subsidiary contracts to the Vatican ever since King John gave England to Pope Innocent III in the 13th century to get back in the good graces of the Pope after being excommunicated. The Papacy *owned* England when these King's Charters were issued to the colonists who came to America. This is a historically verifiable fact.

The Declaration of Independence basically nullified any pre-existing ties and contracts with any and all foreign powers, specifically the British Crown. Once the Declaration was acknowledged by France, it became a contract unto itself with two separate parties agreeing on the conditions of the parting document severing all those ties to British control. From a legal standpoint, this would have also included the nullification of the tenets laid out in the Papal Bull of 1493.

Every colony established by the British Crown on U.S. soil was a matter of contract Charters granted to certain families to spread the British Empire and produce more wealth for the Crown with its expansionist policies. The Declaration of Independence also nullified all these Charters as well. In time it was realized by these families who were issued the Charters that the nullification of Charters by the Declaration of Independence had basically cut their financial throats.

The early colonists tried to band together after the Revolutionary War using the Articles of Confederation as the framework for a new government through which all these 13 States could join together in forming a new model of government. When the Constitutional Convention was convened, the attendees were sent to rework and amend these Articles of Confederation. What they did instead was meet in secret for two months and then they came out with a wholly new document – the Constitution. Each of these representatives to the Constitutional Convention had exceeded their authority by creating an entirely new document and new form of government.

If one reads the Constitution in its unratified form with the attached Bill of Rights Amendments, we find a faulty document – at least from the standpoint of the common workingman, who had no say through voting or otherwise at its inception. In 1776, only men who were 21 years old or older and who owned property were allowed to vote. It wasn't until the passage of the 14th Amendment in 1868 that all men born or naturalized in the United States got the right to vote. So, for almost 80 years after the ratification of the Constitution, the only 'We the People' who could vote owned property.

The passage of the 15th Amendment in 1870 gave Blacks the right to vote, but there were many conditions placed on them such as literacy tests and other things designed to keep them out of the polls. In 1920 women were given the right to vote and it wasn't until 1924 that Native Americans were given citizenship and voting rights. For a brief overview of all these things I am posting a link below to a government website on the Voting History in America.

https://www.sos.wa.gov/_assets/elections/history-of-voting-in-america-timeline.pdf

As should be seen by the foregoing, the Constitution was not established for the common man. It was set up by the elite landowners for the elite landowners. From the time the

Declaration of Independence was written until the Constitution was ratified, 13 years had lapsed. Once the Constitution was written in its original format – having no Bill of Rights attached to it, the propaganda war in the press began between the Federalists and the Anti-federalists. You can thank the Anti-federalists for most of the Bill of Rights amendments to the Constitution.

Now here is where it gets interesting and the illusion over the Constitution gets busted. The Charter owners granted by the British Crown needed to get their licenses back, but how could this be done since they were nullified by the Declaration of Independence? This is where the Contract Clause found in the Constitution comes in. The provision in the Constitution in Article 1 Section 10 in its original form states that "There shall be no law impairing the obligation of contracts", which prevents States from passing laws that nullify pre-existing contracts. With this one clause in the Constitution, all those King's Charters and the Papal Bull were put right back in place and all the Charter holders got their land rights back.

The Federal Constitution is a *corporate* document. It is not a government document as so many Americans have been led to believe in the perceptual illusion. The operatives of the 13 original States who attended the Constitutional Convention in Philadelphia created an Agent to serve as arbiter between themselves over commerce disputes. The UNITED STATES is a corporation, plain and simple, in contradistinction to the 'united States' of the Declaration of Independence. The Senate was originally contrived to look out for the interests of the States. The House of Representatives was established so the individual landowners could look out for their own interests, sort of like voting stockholders in the Federal corporation. The office of the President was equivalent to the CEO and was given the power to enforce the decisions legislated by both Houses of Congress, or the right to Veto if it went against the corporation's interests. In the case of conflict between the Legislative and Executive branches, cases involving Constitutional questions could be taken to the Supreme Court, which was the final arbiter over any disputes about Constitutional violations.

Where Americans have been sold the illusion that the Federal enclave is a government 'of, by and for the people', in its original form, it only included the landed classes. The Federal government was set up purely as an arbiter for trade disputes between the States and the landed gentry and was given the power to levy war through possessing a Navy to fight off any foreign invaders who threatened the Principles of the contract – the States. The Federal government was meant to serve as an Agent to its creators, but in time has turned tables on its creators and has expanded its will and power over the entire nation as a singular overlord, often trampling the rights of the States to manage their own affairs and pass their own laws. This Federal Agent was to support itself by levying tariffs on foreign nations to protect the financial interests of the States and the elite landowners and their businesses.

The original 13 States have all the power as the organizing Principles over the Federal Agent, contractually speaking. Every other State that was created after the Constitution was ratified, was allowed a grant of permission to become a State by petition to the Federal Agent. No State was formed after the Constitution was ratified that the Federal government didn't already own through purchase or conquest. The other 37 States were given equal footing in the Federal corporation as voting members within the Congress and providing candidates for office, but it is still a corporation. For those who choose to doubt what I just revealed, I provide the links below for a discussion of the matter.

*Was the Constitution an Economic Document?* By Dr. Soulet Kyanu (2016)

https://www.academia.edu/30057521/Was_the_American_Constitution_an_Economic_Document

*An Economic Interpretation of The Constitution of The United States* by Charles A. Beard

http://people.tamu.edu/~b-wood/GovtEcon/Beard.pdf

The strength of the Constitution lies in the Bill of Rights which the Marxists have been trying to undermine since Karl Marx wrote his manifesto in 1848. Most people are unaware that Marxist influences have been present in the USA for a long time.

The first Trade Union was initiated by a Freemason named Uriah Smith Stevens who was a member of the Kensington Lodge no. 211 in Philadelphia. He formed the first union as a secret society with its own rituals similar to Freemasonic initiations. He was an advocate for the abolition of slavery as well as supporting a form of utopian socialism. See links below for verification.

https://fishermage.blogspot.com/2011/09/great-freemasons-uriah-smith-stephens.html

https://en.wikipedia.org/wiki/Uriah_Smith_Stephens

https://www.britannica.com/biography/Uriah-Smith-Stephens

It is not widely known or taught in U.S. history courses that the Abolitionist, John Brown, who led the murderous assault at Harpers Ferry was a devoted Marxist, and the Communists still honor his memory today as the one individual who helped precipitate the Civil War. Frederick Douglass, a compatriot of Brown in the most radical wing of the Abolitionist movement is noted for saying after the Civil War:

*"If John Brown did not end the war that ended slavery, he did, at least, begin the war that ended slavery. If we look over the dates, places, and men for which this honor is claimed, we shall*

*find that not Carolina, but Virginia, not Fort Sumter, but Harpers Ferry and the arsenal, not Major Anderson, but John Brown began the war that ended American slavery."*

For verification that the commies still honor Brown visit the website below for the International Communist League.

https://www.icl-fi.org/english/wv/946/brown.html

What I have personally found to be the most comprehensive work on Freemasonry and Marxism in America is a book produced by Arthur S. Thompson, the CEO of the John Birch Society entitled, *To The Victor Go The Myths & Monuments: The History of the First 100 Years of the War Against God and the Constitution, 1776 - 1876, and Its Modern Impact.* This is a massive body of work being 821 pages in length yet affordably priced, and if any reader cares, I give it my personal endorsement as a primary source book in these matters. Link below for those interested. I am not a member of the John Birch Society nor do I have any financial interest in whether this book is purchased or not, I am only sharing it as an extremely good historical reference book.

https://www.jbs.org/store/shopjbs/books/to-the-victor-go-the-myths-and-monuments-1916

I may have strayed a bit from the chapter title, but the fact is that until the average citizen starts to stand up and take an active role in their governing bodies at all levels, meaning doing more than simply voting for your favorite lawyer or charismatic demagogue every two or four years, there is no such thing as We the People. There are only tribal mobs marshaling themselves against all comers who disagree with their particular political ideology. On one hand we have the Christian elements of the culture who still believe that the Constitution is about God, yet the word God is not to be found anywhere in that corporate document. Thomas Jefferson, the author of the Declaration of Independence was not a Christian, he was a Freemason and a Deist, as was George Washington and others who framed the Constitution.

Although the 1st Amendment to the Constitution protects freedom of speech and freedom of the press, it does not offer these same protections for sedition. This was clearly ruled on by the Supreme Court in the *Gitlow v New York* case. This court decision can be viewed at the link below:

https://supreme.justia.com/cases/federal/us/268/652/

Where the lines have been blurred in America today is where communist agitators hide behind the First Amendment's freedom of speech provisions and wrongly interpret freedom of speech to mean freedom of actions. Antifa thugs have no freedom of speech protections when they throw urine bombs and milkshakes mixed with cement on those they disagree with.

Freedom of speech does not extend to clubbing other people, throwing bricks at them or performing acts of property damage. The communists are expert at blurring these lines and their fellow traveler communist judges allow these actions by erroneously ruling that these 'actions' are 'protected speech' through their bullshit interpretations of the law.

The provisions against subversive acts not being protected by the First Amendment also applies when the controlled mainstream media can assault the presidency of the United States and fabricate false conspiracy narratives and broadcast them far and wide 24/7 seeking to unseat a lawfully elected President, yet this subversive activity by communist sympathizers in the mainstream media has been ongoing for almost three years. When we have communist sympathizers in Congress who have sworn an Oath to uphold the Constitution working to undermine and support such activities by violent leftist organizations, then they are also guilty of subversive activities, if not outright treason. The freedoms granted in the Bill of Rights only apply to American citizens. Not subversive assholes whose only dream is to destroy this nation. This includes loudmouth Hollywood stars who spew their communist venom on the airwaves daily. I will discuss Hollywood in a subsequent chapter.

For the first time in American history we have a President of the United States 'corporation' who is a businessman and knows the corporate nature of the document. We finally have someone at the helm who knows how to act like a CEO instead of a political puppet dancing to the whims of the Freemasonic

Marxist occult goddess worshippers. Whether you can accept these facts or not is totally up to you. You are completely free to continue to live the illusion as may be your choice, but it won't alter the truth of the reality revealed in this chapter. If there is ever going to be a genuine We the People, then the people need to get off their asses and start protecting their own interests instead of leaving their lives to be dictated by communists, lawyers and the monied classes who are all dancing in lockstep to the Globalist fiddle. Until the general population takes this course of action, then things will continue as they always have and the illusion of We the People will continue to be nothing more than an illusionary myth in the fantasy world of false perceptions.

# 9. The Scam Called Psychology

As I wrote in earlier chapters, the Greek word *psyche* means 'soul'. The original studies into the field of psychology started through investigations into the supernatural with channelers/mediums who claimed to be able to talk to the spirits of the dead. In ancient times this was considered a form of necromancy or raising the dead from the grave so they could be spoken with and one could allegedly glean their secrets. I covered the abuse of modern psychology in depth in my book, *The Psychology of Becoming Human.*

Modern illusionary perceptions of psychology as well as its practice are so far removed from the investigations into the soul that there is no comparison to its origins and the lies about psychology being peddled to the public. This is not just my perception but is also found in a book by a former psychologist, Ron Roberts, entitled *Psychology and Capitalism: The Manipulation of Mind.* Psychology is a scam!

After years of experimentation based on Pavlov's behavioral experimentation with dogs, psychology was found to be a very effective weapon to shape public perceptions. It started with magazine and newspaper ads, and once radio was invented, the efforts to control public perceptions really escalated. With the creation of talking movies and television, through which images could be placed on the screen accompanied with suggestive narratives, one of the greatest brainwashing tools for the masses was finally realized. In past centuries, stained glass images and art served as the visual mechanism through which religious mind control was reinforced.

In my previous works I have written extensively about a predatory and parasitic mind virus I refer to as the hapiym virus. I have produced no shortage of evidence to support my contentions, particularly in my books *The Energetic War Against Humanity*; *Gutting Mysticism*, and most recently in *The Truth About the 'Divine' Soul.* Since the thrust of this book is designed to explain the world of cognitive illusion we all live in, I have decided it prudent to reprint a chapter from *The Psychology of Becoming Human* which covers this in detail.

# The Study and Implementation of Illusion

*"For our present purpose the real is that which is true for all."*

James Sully, 1881

Throughout my body of work, I have emphasized that the world of normal perceptions, what I call the first cognition, is nothing more than a set of agreed upon perceptual illusions. There are those who are naturally going to disagree with this assessment, feeling fully assured that they have a firm grasp on reality as they perceive it. What I am going to show in this chapter is that everyone suffers under a false cognitive premise that what they think is reality, is in fact a massive species illusion.

As noted in the last chapter, the formulators of what became the field of Psychology were involved in research in many different directions than what mainstream perceptions about the profession lead people to believe, and even what is taught in psychology courses glosses over many of these truths about the origin of the profession. This fact alone should prove that, no matter what you may think psychology is, you are only harboring an illusion about the profession supplied to you by others who are intent on keeping this professional illusion in place. If you are a psychologist, you are also suffering from this same illusion if you think practicing psychology really provides any long lasting 'healing' for the human psyche. Practitioners in the field may devise means and methods to help their clients cope in their cultural milieus but giving someone the capability to *cope* with their anxieties and traumas is not healing them. It is only putting band-aid fixes on psychic wounds that can be truly healed in most people. Psychology as it is currently practiced is only a panacea that masquerades as genuine healing.

To start out this chapter, I am going to offer passages from James Sully, an English psychologist who wrote the book, *Illusions: A Psychological Study* in 1881. This particular work by

Sully was commended both by Sigmund Freud as well as the psychologist Wilhelm Wundt. Wundt was classified in a 1991 article survey in *American Psychologist* as the psychologist whose reputation put him in first place regarding "all-time eminence", with William James and Freud running a distant second and third, respectively, based on the ratings of 29 American historians of psychology. The following excerpt comes from the first chapter of Sully's book, and I think it succinctly summarizes the cognitive state of most humans where being told they are living a life of illusions is concerned:

> *"Common sense, knowing nothing of fine distinctions, is wont to draw a sharp line between the region of illusion and that of sane intelligence. To be the victim of an illusion is, in the popular judgment, to be excluded from the category of rational men. The term at once calls up images of stunted figures with ill-developed brains, half-witted creatures, hardly distinguishable from the admittedly insane. And this way of thinking of illusion and its subjects is strengthened by one of the characteristic sentiments of our age. The nineteenth century intelligence plumes itself on having got at the bottom of mediaeval visions and church miracles, and it is wont to commiserate the feeble minds that are still subject to these self-deceptions.*

*According to this view, illusion is something essentially abnormal and allied to insanity. And it would seem to follow that its nature and origin can be best studied by those whose specialty it is to observe the phenomena of abnormal life. Scientific procedure has in the main conformed to this distinction of common sense. The phenomena of illusion have ordinarily been investigated by alienists, that is to say, physicians who are brought face to face with their most striking forms in the mentally deranged.*

*While there are very good reasons for this treatment of illusion as a branch of mental pathology, it is by no means certain that it can be a complete and exhaustive one. Notwithstanding the flattering supposition of common sense, that illusion is essentially an incident in abnormal life, the careful observer knows well enough that the case is far otherwise.*

*There is, indeed, a view of our race diametrically opposed to the flattering opinion referred to above, namely, the humiliating judgment that all men habitually err, or that illusion is to be regarded as the natural condition of mortals. This idea has found expression, not only in the cynical exclamation of the misanthropist that most men are fools, but also in the cry of despair that sometimes breaks from the weary searcher after absolute truth, and from the poet when impressed with the unreality of his early ideals.*

*Without adopting this very disparaging opinion of the intellectual condition of mankind, we must recognize the fact that most men are sometimes liable to illusion. Hardly anybody is always consistently sober and rational in his perceptions and beliefs. A momentary fatigue of the nerves, a little mental excitement, a relaxation of the effort of attention by which we continually take our bearings with respect to the real world about us, will produce just the same kind of confusion of reality and phantasm which we observe in the insane."*

These observations pretty much sum up the general consensus of human thinking. The idea that one is fooled by illusion outside the context of sleight of hand magic, where one is expecting to be confounded by illusions, is not one that most people are going to readily admit when their perception of reality is challenged. No one likes to admit they have been deceived, and they definitely rebel at the idea that, not only have they been deceived, but that they have been willing participants in the deceit and have deceived themselves. No one likes the idea that they are participants in their own self-deceit, and few are willing to admit

114

this deception, even in the face of evidence that proves their perceptions to be deceptive and illusionary. Unfortunately, this is how the entire first cognition reality functions, with an entire species living in a state of self-deception, ruled by presumed authorities who willfully dictate to us what our perceptions of reality should be. Before one can move into being a totally, cognitively free human being, to become human, one must face this most uncomfortable fact.

In further making his observations on illusions, Sully reports:

> *"Our luminous circle of rational perception is surrounded by a misty penumbra of illusion. Common sense itself may be said to admit this, since the greatest stickler for the enlightenment of our age will be found in practice to accuse most of his acquaintance at some time or another of falling into illusion.*
>
> *If illusion thus has its roots in ordinary mental life, the study of it would seem to belong to the physiology as much as to the pathology of mind. We may even go further, and say that in the analysis and explanation of illusion the psychologist may be expected to do more than the physician. If, on the one hand, the latter has the great privilege of observing the phenomena in their highest intensity, on the other hand, the*

*former has the advantage of being familiar with the normal intellectual process which all illusion simulates or caricatures. To this it must be added that the physician is naturally disposed to look at illusion mainly, if not exclusively, on its practical side, that is, as a concomitant and symptom of cerebral disease, which it is needful to be able to recognize. The psychologist has a different interest in the subject. being specially concerned to understand the mental antecedents of illusion and its relation to accurate perception and belief. It is pretty evident, indeed, that the phenomena of illusion form a region common to the psychologist and the mental pathologist, and that the complete elucidation of the subject will need the co-operation of the two classes of investigator."*

What Sully points out here has been a continual bone of contention between psychologists and psychiatrists since the foundation of psychology as a 'science'. The medical camp is thoroughly convinced that the pathways of the conscious mind are able to be measured and categorized through materialistic neuropathological processes, where the psychologists, not generally trained in physical medicine like a psychiatrist, work more from a theoretical basis to aid in soothing mental distress. These competing forces are still at work arguing with each other over supremacy of doctrine as they have been since the founding of psychology. Each side in this battle is vying for superiority of their ideas where psychology is concerned, and a book published in 2004, *Who Owns Psychology*, edited by Ann Casement, is fully illustrative of this continuing battle over psychology. This is the battle line that was drawn as psychology was being created as a theoretical mind science, and this turf war has not changed one iota since the inception of psychology as the offspring of philosophy.

All parties involved have a vested interest in the process of deception where controlling psychology is concerned, and why humans fall prey so easily to trusting it. To most, deception constitutes lying or some form of confidence scheme where one is unwittingly deceived to their detriment. Few indeed have the wherewithal to contemplate the notion that the majority of their perceptions of reality are contrived and doled out to them by people who know how to manipulate human perceptions after a century's worth of psychological observations and questionable, hidden experimentation practices. Sully's examination of illusions from a psychological study standpoint has high relevance in our modern world where, contrary to popular opinion, virtually our every thought is controlled by one form of illusion or another. As Sully notes below, there is a hairline distinction between what we consider our normal perceptions and those of the abnormal variety, which are more highly pronounced illusions in the mind of the mentally unbalanced.

*"Indeed, it will be found that the two groups of phenomena—**the illusions of the normal and of the abnormal condition—are so similar, and pass into one another by such insensible gradations, that it is impossible to discuss the one apart from the other**. The view of illusion which will be adopted in this work is that it constitutes a kind of borderland between perfectly sane and vigorous mental life and dementia.*

*And here at once there forces itself on our attention the question. **What exactly is to be understood by the term " illusion"? In scientific works treating of the pathology of the subject, the word is confined to what are specially known as illusions of the senses, that is to say, to false or illusory perceptions.** And there is very good reason for this limitation, since such illusions of the senses are the most palpable and striking symptoms of mental disease. In addition to this, it must be allowed that, **to the ordinary reader, the term first of all calls up this same idea of a deception of the senses.***

*At the same time, popular usage has long since extended the term so as to include under it errors which do not counterfeit actual perceptions. We commonly speak of a man being under an illusion respecting himself when he has a ridiculously exaggerated view of his own importance, and in a similar way of a person being in a state of illusion with respect to the past when, through frailty of memory, he pictures it quite otherwise than it is certainly known to have been.*

*It will be found, I think, that there is a very good reason for this popular extension of the term.* **The errors just alluded to have this in common with illusions of sense, that they simulate the form of immediate or self-evident cognition. An idea held respecting ourselves or respecting our past history does not depend on any other piece of knowledge; in other words, is not adopted as the result of a process of reasoning.** *What I believe with reference to my past history, so far as I can myself recall it, I believe instantaneously and immediately, without the intervention of any premise or reason. Similarly, our notions of ourselves are, for the most part, obtained apart from any process of inference. The view which a man takes of his own character or claims on society he is popularly supposed to receive intuitively by a mere act of internal observation. Such beliefs may not, indeed, have all the overpowering force which belongs to illusory perceptions, for the intuition of something by the senses is commonly looked on as the most* *immediate and irresistible kind of knowledge. **Still,** **they must be said to come very near illusions of** **sense in the degree of their self-evident certainty.***

*As we proceed, we shall, I think, find an ample justification for our definition. We shall see that **such illusions as those respecting ourselves** **or the past arise by very much the same mental** **processes as those which are discoverable in the** **production of illusory perceptions;** and thus a complete psychology of the one class will, at the same time, contain the explanation of the other classes.*

*The reader is doubtless aware that philosophers have still further extended the idea of illusion by seeking to bring under it **beliefs which** **the common sense of mankind has always** **adopted and never begun to suspect.** Thus, according to the idealist, the popular notion (the existence of which Berkeley, however, denied) of an external world, existing in itself and in no wise dependent on our perceptions of it, resolves itself into a grand illusion of sense. "*

[Bold emphasis mine]

Sully's observations here about unquestioned illusions are highly pertinent to this discussion, particularly those illusions we each harbor about ourselves and who we think we are. We do not realize that we are, as a rule, *programmed* by our cultures, our educational systems, our religions and our beliefs of all kinds. We are unwilling to accept the idea that our cultural heritage may be nothing more than a sanitized historical myth which bolsters our individual sense of national or cultural pride. The external psychological programming every human is subjected to controls their psyches down to the level of their perceived individual identity. This personal identity, the false personality of the ego, provided by the effects of the hapiym mind virus, create every facet of our perceptual reality. In truth, none of us are really who we think we are. We are all living a life of illusionary perception, and this is why Sully's work is of such great import to this study. Until the practicing psychologist is willing to admit that they are just as affected by the mind virus as their clients, then their own sense of denial will blind them from ever truly understanding the 'human condition'.

In its formative years, when psychology was being molded into what it is today, *everything* was being investigated where its impact on the mind was concerned. Researchers puzzled over the deception of optical illusions, with no time spared in experimentation on optical psychology. Other researchers like William James and investigators from both sides of the spectrum, believers and skeptics alike, studied the Spiritism of the 19th century to understand its effects on the human psyche, with one side wanting them validated and the other wanting the testimonies of mediums removed as any measure of materialist science. This competition and conflict are catalogued very capably in Michael

Pettit's book, *The Science of Deception: Psychology and Commerce in America.*

For over half a century, as psychology was being shaped into the discipline and profession it has become today, every aspect of human perceptions was studied, from artificially induced hypnotic trance states produced in the laboratory to the self-induced trance states of mediums and Eastern yogis and Tibetan monks. Each school of thought, both the medical and scientific, as well as the more esoteric and philosophical framers of psychology, had a specific agenda in shaping the new 'science', and the competition for who would ultimately control the 'New Psychology' was fierce indeed. This competition has not lessened over the decades.

Where Sully's work bears importance in this volume in his observations in *Illusions* can be summarized in part by the following passage:

*"It appears at first as if the preliminary stages — the reception, discrimination, and classification of an impression—would not offer the slightest opening for error. This part of the mechanism of perception seems to work so regularly and so smoothly that one can hardly conceive a fault in the process. Nevertheless, a little consideration will show that even here all does not go on with unerring precision.*

*Let us suppose that **the very first step is wanting distinct attention to an impression. It is easy to see that this will favour illusion by leading to a confusion of the impression.***"

[Bold italics mine]


What sustains the first cognition world of perceptual reality, as the emphasized section above points out, is the wanting, or desire for something to be true. One could call this desire for something to be true nothing more than simple belief. Through classical conditioning, which starts in all of us in childhood, we are all conditioned to believe the rules of our cultures. This indoctrination, or programming as I call it, sets the stage for creating within us a form of herd compliance within our own cultural mandates. Once we have this programming in place, then we develop expectations about what we want to be true about our given cultures and how we individually fit into this herd structure. We are then programmed with our culture's traditions and history, which creates more expectations and also shapes our primary personality to conform with these cultural herd norms. Once we accept these ideas, then we are all more prone to fall for the illusions presented to us on an individual basis so long as the illusions conform to our primary cultural herd programming. We develop a desire for certain things to be true, and this is based on whether any given illusion or perception can be molded to conform to our sensory impressions about ourselves and our cultures, religions, political ideologies, or national identity.

Through such programming, based on cultural mandates and societal norms, we then become part of the herd. The Yaqui shaman don Juan referred to this point of becoming part of the herd as the point at which we gain our 'membership' in the cultural fellowship. When we attain this membership, any sense of true individuality we may have had as young children is now replaced with the identity of our respective cultural herds. Our personal identity is gauged by how well we fit into the herd milieu. We are no longer autonomous individuals, we are now herd animals.

When someone has the availability and resources to influence our perceptions, then a perceptual reality can be woven into our psyches through the process of herd inculcation, by creating a 'consensus reality'. As Napoleon accurately noted, "History is an agreed upon set of lies." As far back as recorded human history goes, as a species we have been governed by an agreed upon set of lies from one culture to the next. All of these lies take the form of beliefs, whether true or untrue, that are agreed upon and enforced by every cultural herd. It is this nature of herd conformity and herd compliance that is the signature of the hapiym mind virus and how it has poisoned our species psyche. I will not disagree with the concept that human beings like social intercourse, but what has occurred under the influence of the hive virus is that this basic level of socialization has been artificially amplified through the virus infection and, as a result of the infection, scarcely a human being alive today can truly walk alone or independent from any given herd. The very idea of being alone and unaccepted is utterly frightening to most human beings.

What I contend in this presentation is the concept that our entire social structure worldwide has been influenced by this mind virus, and that humanity in general is acting according to the mandates of this virus and those humans on this planet who worked in collusion with the hive intelligences to create a reality based entirely on belief and illusion. What humanity perceives as reality is nothing more than culturally accepted beliefs passed from generation to generation to keep the consciousness of our entire species enslaved to the needs of the hapiym virus. We are all bound to living a world of illusion predicated on these varied beliefs, and as such, what we perceive as reality is in actuality an artfully contrived illusion to which we all willingly and ignorantly submit to out of our cultural herd programming. We are all active participants in the illusion we call reality, and many would rather die to defend this illusion than admit the ghastly horror of it all.

One of the least understood philosophers of all time is Friedrich Nietzsche. Although he sits at the fringes of philosophy because he didn't conform much to any one philosophical ideology, his works have had a profound effect in certain elite circles, particularly within the field of psychology, influencing the likes of Sigmund Freud, Alfred Adler and Carl Jung. Unfortunately, none of these pillars of psychology had any genuine understanding of what he tried to teach humanity.

In his book *Ecce Homo*, Nietzsche truthfully stated:

*"That a psychologist without equal speaks from my writings – this is perhaps the first insight gained by a good reader."*

*"Who among the philosophers before me was in any way a psychologist? Before me there simply was no psychology"*

Truer words were never spoken where the field of psychology is concerned, and unfortunately, there is not a single psychologist, living or dead, who understood what he taught. Where psychologists all strive to look into the minds of others, there are none who even understand the workings of their own mind to make any kind of genuine value judgment on the workings within the minds of their clients. It was exactly because Nietzsche plumbed the depths of his own psyche that he became the brilliant observer that he was. He reached a totally different level of perception and understanding that first cognition psychologists can barely reach. He bridged the gap between the limited perceptions of the first cognition illusion and stepped into the higher-level state of awareness I call the second cognition.

One of his least understood essays, from *Untimely Meditations*, is entitled *The Use and Abuse of History for Life*. I am going to take this opportunity to explain this mysterious piece of work to philosophers and psychologists alike who study Nietzsche, to clarify and translate what he meant when he wrote that essay. As will be shown, this essay folds perfectly into this chapter on manipulating illusions and how it is done wholesale to our species and our individual psyches. He opens the essay as follows:

*"Incidentally, I despise everything which merely instructs me without increasing or immediately enlivening my activity." These are Goethe's words. With them, as with a heartfelt expression of Ceterum censeo [I judge otherwise], our consideration of the worth and the worthlessness of history may begin. For this work is to set down why, in the spirit of Goethe's saying, we must seriously despise instruction without vitality, knowledge which enervates activity, and history as an expensive surplus of knowledge and a luxury, because we lack what is still most essential to us and because what is superfluous is hostile to what is essential. To be sure, we need history. But we need it in a manner different from the way in which the spoilt idler in the garden of knowledge uses it, no matter how elegantly he may look down on our coarse and graceless needs and distresses. That is, we need it for life and action, not for a comfortable turning away from life and action or merely for glossing over the egotistical life and the cowardly bad act. We wish to use history only insofar as it serves living. But **there is a degree of doing history and a valuing of it through which life atrophies and degenerates**. To*

*bring this phenomenon to light as a remarkable symptom of our time is every bit as necessary as it may be painful.*

[Bold emphasis mine]


With history at present being nothing more than agreed upon sets of lies accepted by cultural populations at large as their mythical heritage, history has been abused to create cultural illusions. The selective and sanitized reporting of history creates a form of herd solidarity, peppered with the required national, cultural or religious heroes which lend credence to the cultural mythology. These cultural heroes create within their respective herds, something to which the individual inner personality feels it can aspire, and therefore become one of the herd heroes as well. When any group of people can control the cultural narrative, then a perceptual illusion is woven to deceive the consciousness of the recipients of such doctrines. This, I assert, is what has taken place within the psyche of all humanity. This is part of the great illusion we call reality, and because we believe it within our cultural herds, we will defend this illusion against all comers who challenge the illusion as false. We beg to not only be deceived by these illusions, but we become allies of the deceivers by embracing and defending the illusions as reality. This is, in actuality, how crowd psychology is abused to control the masses by a handful of elite controllers whose only agenda is to rule the planet and return humanity to a state of oligarchic feudalism. This manipulation is well documented and can be readily verified with diligent research. It is not an unsupported claim.

It is this contrived manipulation of sanitizing history to control these cultural myths to create herd mindsets and beliefs, that creates the atrophy and life defeating uses of history Nietzsche warned about. As much as Nietzsche tried to bring this truth to light in his lifetime, his messages were unheeded, and humanity is still moving inexorably downward, living their lives defending their personal identities as part of their cultural identities, shaping the perception of who they are based on false beliefs called history. Facing this truth is no less painful for the hapiym-controlled human psyche today than it was during Nietzsche's lifetime, yet this is a necessary element in the psychology of becoming human. As Nietzsche observes:

> *"This essay is also out of touch with the times because here I am trying for once to see as a contemporary disgrace, infirmity, and defect something of which our age is justifiably proud, its historical culture. **For I believe, in fact, that we are all suffering from a consumptive historical fever and at the very least should recognize that we are afflicted with it.**"*

Relying on sanitized and falsified history is definitely a cognitive affliction when the reliance and belief on the cultural myths shape the very essence of who we think we are within that cultural and historical framework, and there is no human being within their respective cultures that escapes this historical affliction. Nietzsche further writes:

> *"Observe the herd which is grazing beside you. It does not know what yesterday or today is. It springs around, eats, rests, digests, jumps up again, and so from morning to night and from day to day, with its likes and dislikes closely tied to the peg of the moment, and thus neither melancholy nor weary. To witness this is hard for man, because he boasts to himself that his human race is better than the beast and yet looks with jealousy at its happiness. For he wishes only to live like the beast, neither weary nor amid pains, and he wants it in vain, because he does not will it as the animal does. One day the man demands of the beast: "Why do you not talk to me about your happiness and only gaze at me?" The beast wants to answer, too, and say: "That comes about because I always immediately forget what I wanted to say." But by then the beast has already forgotten this reply and remains silent, so that the man wonders on once more.*
> *But he also wonders about himself, **that he is not able to learn to forget and that he always hangs onto past things. No matter how far or how***

*fast he runs, this chain runs with him. It is something amazing: the moment, in one sudden motion there, in one sudden motion gone, before nothing, afterwards nothing, nevertheless comes back again as a ghost and disturbs the tranquility of each later moment. A leaf is continuously released from the roll of time, falls out, flutters away—and suddenly flutters back again into the man's lap. For the man says, "I remember," and envies the beast, which immediately forgets and sees each moment really perish, sink back in cloud and night, and vanish forever.*

*Thus the beast lives unhistorically, for it gets up in the present like a number without any odd fraction left over; it does not know how to play a part, hides nothing, and appears in each moment exactly and entirely what it is. Thus a beast can be nothing other than honest. By contrast, **the human being resists the large and ever increasing burden of the past, which pushes him down or bows him over. It makes his way difficult, like an invisible and dark burden which he can for appearances' sake even deny, and which he is only too happy to deny in his interactions with his peers, in order to awaken their envy.** Thus, it moves him, as if he remembered a lost paradise, to see the grazing herd or, something more closely familiar, **the*** *child, which does not yet have a past to deny and plays in blissful blindness between the fences of the past and the future. Nonetheless this game must be upset for the child. He will be summoned all too soon out of his forgetfulness. For he learns to understand the expression "It was," that password with which struggle, suffering, and weariness come over human beings, so as to remind him what his existence basically is—a never completed past tense. If death finally brings the longed for forgetting, it nevertheless thereby destroys present existence and thus impresses its seal on the knowledge that **existence is only an uninterrupted living in the past** [Gewesensein], **something which exists for the purpose of self-denial, self-destruction, and self-contradiction.***"*

[All emphasis mine]

With this passage we arrive at the crux of the problem where living the illusion is concerned with our historical beliefs. As a species, as Nietzsche notes, we are chained to the past. If you seriously ponder about who you think you are, you will see that you are a collection of beliefs and incidents called 'the past'. One can never live cognitively free and in the now, as Nietzsche points to as the behavior of the beasts, because we are constantly measuring ourselves under the weight of the historical illusions that shape the individual identity. Whether it is cultural histories of all kinds, or our personal histories, everything we do today is measured by the past. The entire human race is chained to the past to make almost any decision we make as individuals. As such, we are caught in an ever-building heap of history of which we are only leaves on the wind to blow with the herd influence of that past.

The hapiym virus created a false persona that attached to our primary sense of self-identity, the basic ego, or waking self. Once infected, the virus starts creating a world of illusion around itself, mimicking the primary personality of the basic ego, and turning it into a monster by overlaying our primary instincts with the illusionary world of the virus. This concocted world of programmed illusions is so powerful that the virus eventually convinces us that the virus truly *is* us, and we accept that premise without question all our lives. To reach the state of becoming truly human, with a totally free consciousness, one must face the truthfulness about these illusions, and one must overcome the illusions in order to be free of them. Until this process is met and accomplished, as Nietzsche himself did, one is nothing but a facsimile of a human, a virus-generated false personality which is just as illusionary as the world in which the virus thrived and grew. Before psychology can ever become a truly effective healing discipline, it will have to face these truths and, when these truths are accepted, and the psychologist can transcend their own false mental persona created by the virus, will the science truly turn into a science for healing human consciousness and not speculative theory catering to nurturing the habits of the virus resident in the human psyche.

This attachment to history in a personal sense can be exemplified with the emphasis on nostalgia, where the individual gets stuck in their 'glory days' and can't seem to let go of identifying who they are now with who they were 'back in the day'. Through the intentional promotion of nostalgia by means of radio stations playing the 'oldies but goodies', the cognitive programming that keeps people stuck in the past is very evident when one's attention is drawn to this fact.

People are controlled through their emotions and lead with their emotions. This emphasis on nostalgia and the yearning for a better time, or what we presume was a better time in our lives, keeps these chains to the past firmly in place and it supports the false persona of the virus, which fed on the output from human emotions. The music, television and film industries have been highly manipulated and controlled in order to ensure that the cultural illusions of the past live on and are perpetuated as controlling factors in our psyche. They have been used as powerful weapons of psychological control with a power as yet unadmitted by the public at large.

We must step back and take a look at the fictional world of the *Matrix* to really comprehend the magnitude of that machine-generated illusion and compare it to the massive perceptual illusions that truly keep our consciousness chained and unchanging in the world we inhabit. Our species continually repeats the past because, on a cognitive level, it can't stop living that past long enough to find an exit away from the historical chains that keep our consciousness locked into the same patterns of thinking generation after generation. It is specifically due to recognizing these patterns in thinking and behavior that Crowd Psychology works as a mechanism for controlling societies worldwide. When you can control the perceptions you control the illusion, no matter what shape it takes, then you control the herds who believe the illusion to be real.

Religions and ancient kings figured out thousands of years ago how to control their herds through emotional manipulation, most notably with fear. The authoritarian leaders had all the power, and if they were displeased with you enough, death was often the penalty for going against their will. It is fear today that controls people trapped in the illusions, the fear of admitting that their perception of life has been nothing but a series of lies, and that they have deceived themselves by agreeing with the perceptual lies. The fear of admitting this is the greatest fear any human must face before they can begin to set themselves free from the illusion.

So long as any particular herd illusion makes one feel good emotionally, the illusion can be fully embraced. If it makes one feel comfortable in their feeling good about their illusionary beliefs, then their willingness to listen to anything that disrupts this comfort and makes them stop feeling good with their illusion, gives rise to the fight or flight mechanism, where one will either fight to defend the belief, or simply run away from the truth and deny it.

Within any given herd association, be it religion, nationality, traditions, political ideologies or spirituality, confirmation bias is what supports the illusion. Each of these are sustained by superficial illusions and the thing called *belief*. If you scratch the surface of any of the things that hold selective human herds together, you will find that there is little to no truth to sustain the beliefs. At the very best, one may find half-truths, but half a truth is still half a lie. Within the perceptual illusions of our reality, we are driven by hope and fear, the hope that tomorrow will be better, and the fear that it might not. These two emotions create a roller coaster of ups and downs in our psyche and generate a lot of emotional energy, which was the food supply of the hapiym virus. The virus would soothe us with feel-good beliefs which produced the emotions of well-being, so it could feed, and it would use fear against us if we were ever confronted with any information that destroyed or challenged its world of illusion. Hope is the carrot, and fear is the stick that keeps the human psyche in line with the herd mandates of the mental hive virus.

Modern institutional Buddhism is a far cry from the pure teachings of Siddhartha Guatama, the original Buddha. Buddha, like Nietzsche, had attained the second cognition state of awareness and he tried to teach it to humanity. In line with the subject matter in this chapter on illusion, Buddha taught:

*Those who take the non-real for the real*
*and the real for the non-real and thus fall victims*
*to erroneous notions never reach the essence of*

*reality. Having realised the essential as the essential and the non-essential as the non-essential, they by thus following correct thinking attain the essential. --- Dhammapada (11-12)*

The 'essential' referred to in this passage is the second cognition state of awareness, which deals with reality and pragmatism, the real over the non-real. Unless and until one is willing to challenge all the illusions, both in the external world as well as our internal world, then one will remain trapped in the world of the non-real, never knowing or seeing reality, forever trapped in the illusion until they choose to break free of it and finally become fully human, and not just a facsimile of one operating under the residual effects of the hapiym virus and its false persona.

I realize that this was a very lengthy chapter but given the subject matter of the overall presentation of this book, I felt it necessary to bring these comprehensive facts to light.

Psychology as it is practiced and sold today is a far cry from its origins where the Greek philosophers worked with their internal hive cells, which they referred to as *dæmons*. Christians later turned the word into demons, but both descriptions defined the same phenomenon. Psychology is a scam, pure and simple. It is a weapon for mind control and reinforcing herd cultural compliance. It is nothing more than another illusionary *product* in the modern marketplace, no different than religion and spirituality being just *products* to their believers. It's all part of the Grand Illusion.

# 10. Revival of an Ancient War

What humanity is witnessing at this time that goes beyond the perceptions of the fantasy world of illusion is the revival of an ancient conflict. After the Age of Enlightenment philosophers sought to reduce the world to materialist mechanics, we saw the rise of the Romance philosophers who were more interested in emotions, love and particularly, goddess worship.

In biblical traditions, the Jewish God Yahweh, who was only one of many regional or tribal gods throughout the Fertile Crescent, was always at war with his Pagan adversaries, particularly the followers of the goddess cults – notably Asherah, Ashtoreth, Astarte, also known as Ishtar. It was these goddesses (actually one goddess who went by many names in many lands) against whom the Levitical followers of Yahweh waged incessant and tireless war. This war never ended, but the goddess worshippers were driven underground time and again, only to reappear once again in our modern era.

In its last permutation before the Renaissance Era and the subsequent Romantic era a few centuries later, the formulators of the Christian ideology were in a hammer and tong conflict with the Egyptian cult of Isis. Had the violence of the Christian mobs not held the upper hand, we would be worshipping Isis today. The goddess made her reappearance with the French Revolution as the goddess Liberty, leading the proletariat over the dead bodies of those who stood against her revolutionary spirit. As I reported in earlier chapters, the being called Lucifer worshipped by the Freemasons is an allegorical representation of the Goddess with 1,000 names. In Ancient Greece this goddess represented both sexes found in the god Hermes and the goddess Aphrodite, who were eventually merged into the hybrid bisexual god Hermaphroditus. The goddess against whom Yahweh warred was a goddess of sexual revelry, drunkenness, prostitution and abandon, who herself was a hermaphrodite. It is from the god Hermaphroditus that we get the word hermaphrodite. I covered this extensively in *Gutting Mysticism* as well as in *Religion, the Goddess and the Mind Virus of Heaven: The Deception of Holiness in Human Belief Systems.*

Much of the so-called sexual revolution that started in the 1960s was part of this modern revival of these ancient goddess cults, most often associated with mystery religions and rituals such as the Eleusinian Mysteries. Such mysteries are also found in the cult of the sun god Mithras, and even early Christianity was considered one of these mystery cults, as much as modern Christians may wish to dispute these readily verifiable facts.

The orders of Freemasonry revere the star Sirius, and the star Sirius is associated with the goddess Isis. This is the basis for the women's Freemasonic auxiliary organization, The Eastern Star. In Judaism this goddess is known as the consort of Yahweh and is referred to as the Shekinah. The son of Isis was Horus, represented by the All-seeing Eye which sits hovering above the top of the Freemasonic pyramid and is found on the back of the U.S. Dollar bill. Both the cult of Mithra and the Zoroastrian god Ahura Mazda were solar gods. The Persian Ahura Mazda was only a variant of the Egyptian Horus.

The god Osiris, in Egyptian legend, was murdered by his brother Seth, and it goes beyond the scope of this book to delve into that story in full, with all its mythological permutations. Briefly, as the story goes, after Seth (or Set) killed Osiris, Isis was able to revive Osiris after his body had been cut into 14 pieces and she gave him a magical penis (which had been swallowed by an *oxyrinchus* fish), from which she was able to give birth to Horus. Because Osiris had been murdered, Isis was always referred to as the widow. This is why all Freemasons refer to themselves as Sons of the Widow – they are secret followers of Isis.

In Greek religious lore it is the goddess Hecate that is the guardian of the gates between the underworld and heaven and who has the ability to transport souls either way. Hecate's brother/son Hermes also has this magical ability to transport souls to their final destination. The Statue of Liberty in New York Harbor was a gift from French Freemasons to the Freemasonic lodges in America. Some call her the goddess Columbia, whose symbol is also found as the logo for Columbia Pictures. The seven prongs on the crown of the statue are also representative of the goddess Hecate, who was often portrayed wearing a seven-rayed crown.

The seven rays are found deeply embedded in the writings of the Theosophical Society and have several meanings. In one case they represent the rays of the Sun. In other interpretations they represent the primary colors of the rainbow, which is why you see the rainbow colors representing the LGBTQ movement as well as other faux spiritual and subversive leftist organizations. The number seven was sacred to the goddess and is also representative of the planet Saturn, from whose wanton festivals the Roman celebrated as Saturnalia, which the Greeks called Bacchanalia.

In certain ancient traditions Isis claimed to be the eldest daughter of Saturn. Saturn is also associated with the black cube, and the word Ka'aba, the center of Islamic pilgrimage site at Mecca is a derivation of the Anatolian goddess name Cybele, who was married to Saturn (Kronos) In ancient times cube-shaped stones were used to honor this goddess. The black cubes representing Saturn are worn for prayer ceremonies on the heads of the Hasidic Jews, which are called *teffilin*. It is from Saturn's Day that we get the word Saturday, the 7th day of the week. It should also be noted that Saturday is the Sabbath day of the Jews. Are the coincidences starting to pile up here yet?

For these who have been doing research and paying attention, they have noticed a large number of black cube statues erected around the world. For proof of these just look up *Black Cube Statues* on Google to see the examples.

https://www.google.com/search?sxsrf=ACYBGNSgHNB EzIdbtdOlaZoRo9ghk3gAmw:1567717555535&q=black+cube+ statues&tbm=isch&source=univ&client=avast&sxsrf=ACYBGN

SgHNBEzIdbtdOlaZoRo9ghk3gAmw:1567717555535&sa=X&
ved=2ahUKEwiMuIWAy7rkAhVFPq0KHW9oCg4QsAR6BAg
HEAE&biw=1159&bih=589

When Muslims do their pilgrimage to Mecca, they are expected to circumambulate around the black cube in Mecca counterclockwise seven times, as some suggest, emulating the rings of Saturn. If one picks one corner of a cube as a starting point, then they will discover that there are seven lines, or rays that emanate from that point. For an illustrated example of this look up *The Gnostic Jesus The Invisible Sun Behind the Sun* or see the link below. Just scroll down a bit and see the image of the cube on the left.

http://www.plotinus.com/gnostic_jesus_copy.htm

For a more comprehensive presentation about *Cybele, Rhea, Isis, and the Black Cube Mother*, look up that title on YouTube or see the link below. The music in the video gets kind of irritating so you may want to dispense with listening as most of the information is presented in pictures and text anyway.

https://www.youtube.com/watch?v=SAw4ji5ZNiI

So, what does all this mean regarding living in the fantasy world of illusion? How much of this did you know? How much of this have you even questioned or paid attention to? Are we to believe it is accidental that Christianity's day of worship is Sun Day? Are we to ignore the fact that when Constantine won his battle at the Milvian Bridge that he was given a sign that he would win the day using the symbol of Sol Invictus, the conquering Sun? Although Christian mythology has altered this myth to say that Constantine saw the vision of the Cross, I prefer to buy the former argument that he conquered in the name of the Sun as he had not yet adopted Christianity and mandated it as the State religion. Any stories to the contrary are merely Christian propaganda written after the fact.

I have written exhaustively on these subjects in *Gutting Mysticism* and am not going to recount everything here that I reported in that volume. The point of sharing this now is to illustrate that there is no linkage between Judaism as it is practiced by the Rabbis and the Christianity of the New Testament. The concept of 'Judeo-Christian' traditions is another cognitive illusion that falls apart once it is seriously analyzed. Judaism is a monotheistic system of belief, Christianity is a trinitarian system of belief based on religious tenets provided by the hermaphrodite goddess represented by the Father (Osiris), Son (Horus) and Holy Spirit (Mother Mary – the Queen of Heaven). Any concerted study into all the religions of the world show them all to be nothing but illusionary systems of belief (and that includes the religion of Marxist Socialism). As much as the reader may protest and wish to run me down for making these assertions I will ask you this – have you done any of the research that can effectively refute the research I have exhaustively done in the 33 books I have written?

If not, you are only defending an illusion because it either makes you feels good or you fear letting it go.

I don't want the reader believing that I am simply attacking religion. This book is about exposing the *all* the cognitive illusions that keep humanity's consciousness in chains. I had to find and face the truth in everything I revealed in this book and my other works. It hasn't been an easy path for me to come to terms with these things and move past the illusions, nor will it be for anyone who wants to free their mind of the fantasy world of illusions. I had to face the truth about my religion, my spiritual ambitions, my beliefs in historical lies and how I deceived myself in justifying believing the illusions as long as I did. One can either face it or run away from it but running away from the truth only leaves your mind in bondage to the fantasy world of illusion. The fact is, from my personal observations, that most people simply don't want or care about knowing the truth. The illusions are much more satisfying and easier to digest given all the cultural programing we have been subjected to as a species throughout or history.

One of the greatest illusions we are held captive to is the illusion of fiat currency being money. A Federal Reserve Note issued by the Federal Reserve system is not money, it is an instrument of debt. The need for a central bank is one of the 10 planks of Marx's Communist Manifesto, but the House of Rothschild has been in the business of loaning money to governments at interest since before the Napoleonic wars. International bankers of the Rothschild variety sought early on to gain control of the monetary system in the U.S. with the First Bank of the United States.

Like the modern Federal Reserve central banking system, the First Bank of the United States was a privately-owned corporation heavily sponsored by the Federalist Alexander Hamilton. For more information on the bank see Wikipedia under *First Bank of the United States*.

https://en.wikipedia.org/wiki/First_Bank_of_the_United_States

Five years after the 20-year charter of the First Bank was not voted for renewal by the congress, the Second Bank of the United States was put into place for another 20-year charter. It was during a war to prevent the re-chartering of the Second Bank between Andrew Jackson and Bank's president, Nicholas Biddle, that attempted assassinations on President Jackson occurred. See *Second Bank of the United State* at Wikipedia for more information, or a brief article called *Bank War* at History.com for a bit more information. Links below.

https://en.wikipedia.org/wiki/Second_Bank_of_the_United_States

https://www.history.com/topics/19th-century/bank-war

Andrew Jackson won this war against the Second Bank of the United States, and it wasn't until 1913 that Marxist activists sneakily passed the Federal Reserve Act on Dec. 23, 1913 to reinstate another private banking consortium in the United States. The Federal Reserve is no more Federal than Federal Express. It is just one more illusion that most of the public is purely ignorant of. The Federal Reserve Act was passed by three senators who had intentionally remained behind in Washington, D.C. for the Christmas recess of the Senate after all other senators had taken trains home for the holidays. Under Senate rules a bill can be passed by a majority vote of those present, which is exactly how the U.S. got saddled once more with a privately-owned central bank. For a more extensive examination of the backroom deal-making that led to the Fed's creation, see G. Edward Griffin's, *The Creature from Jekyll Island.*

https://archive.org/details/pdfy--Pori1NL6fKm2SnY

The last aspect of the illusion I am going to cover in this volume is the illusion of Hollywood and how it has been infiltrated and controlled by communists. During the 1950s we had what the communist press refers to as McCarthy's 'witch hunt' with his blacklists designed to keep communist filmmakers and actors and actresses out of the workplace. As I reported in an earlier chapter, with the fall of the Iron Curtain and the access to Soviet records, it has been proven that not only was McCarthy on track with his investigations, but that the subversive infiltration of communist agents into Hollywood, the trade unions and high levels of government was substantially more than McCarthy discovered.

Today's Hollywood, presently screaming for blacklisting any and all who vote for President Trump or who contribute to his presidential campaign efforts, are no different than the communist propagandists of old, except these days they are more blatant about their attacks on America and a sitting American President. They have now resorted to using McCarthy's tactics against America at this time. No time in American history, even during the lead up to the Civil War, has any president had to endure such endless assaults from the media, Hollywood and even within our own Congress. One must ask why the commies so fear this president?

Along with the recent revelations about child sex trafficking with the Jeffrey Epstein case, Hollywood moguls, actors and actresses are currently under investigation for sex trafficking in the NXIVM (Nexium) sex scandal. This investigation has not yet seen the full light of day, but it won't be long before telling the public at large. Although Epstein allegedly committed suicide while in a Federal detention center, it will eventually come out that Epstein along with thousands of other elitists worldwide – Great Britain's Prince Andrew, to name just one - have been involved in child sex trafficking and pedophilia. The public is only now being apprised of young girls 14 years and older being involved in these underaged sexual predatory practices. The public is yet to learn that this massive elitist global pedophile ring was also trafficking toddlers and underaged children of both sexes. Investigations into the Clinton Foundation by the Inspector General have leveled accusations of Crimes Against Children by the Clinton Foundation, and I don't believe it will be too long before the massive scope of these crimes is made known to the public at large.

One executive from the Disney corporation has already been convicted of child rape and other court cases have been filed against other Disney executives for similar charges. It will be revealed that the Hollywood and pop music industry is filled with children that have been subjected to CIA MK Ultra mind control practices and sexual exploitation as children. Disney Cruise lines frequented Jeffrey Epstein's 'Lolita Island' for many years. We can only wonder what associations there were between Epstein's pedophile practices and Disney with these things.

One of the primary tactics of communist subversion is to destroy the morals of the countries they infiltrate. With their sworn enemies being Christianity and Capitalism, we must lay an indictment at the feet of Hollywood studios and producers, many of whom are now wholly owned by Chinese communist organizations, for pushing violence, sex and mayhem in their films and TV shows. The same infiltration has taken place in Japanese anime, children's cartoon shows as well as the video game industry to push communist propaganda. Make no mistake, we are facing a massive global assault against our consciousness and cheapening the value of human life, which the communists have never given a hoot for anyway. The murderous history of communism bears out their lack of concern for human life – even those within their own ranks. For more information on the communist infiltration of Hollywood read *Hollywood Traitors: Agents of Stalin Allies of Hitler*. PDF download link below.

https://www.pdfdrive.com/hollywood-traitors-blacklisted-screenwriters-e60604647.html

You might also want to read *Blacklisted by History: The Untold Story of Senator Joe McCarthy and His Fight Against America's Enemies* by M. Stanton Evans if you want to see inverted history turned right side up.

Also look into *American Betrayal: The Secret Assault on Our Nation's Character American Betrayal* by Diana West. Ms. West has suffered no shortage of onslaught by communist academics in her revelations of truth in this book. These books can be purchased at Amazon and other booksellers.

In October 2017 there appeared a mysterious person who simply identified themselves as Q who started posting on some messages boards at a social network called 4Chan. They subsequently moved to an alternate website called 8Chan. This is the foundation for what is known as the Q movement. Q claimed to be part of a military intelligence operation feeding what facts it can to the American public in preparation for the exposure of much of what is contained in this book against the Globalist criminal cabal.

I came to the Q material perhaps eight months after these posts started. The people who follow Q call themselves the Anons.

After my previous investigations into the Jesuit-controlled Anonymous movement, I was highly skeptical of anything relating to Anonymous. It was only after reading some of the posts and watching things predicted in the Q posts start appearing in the mainstream news outlets that I saw the validity in what was being posted. I have become very skeptical in my years of research.

Needless to say, the Qanon movement has become a major thorn in the side of the communist media and the press has spared no shortage of ink to shut down and silence the Q movement. You have to ask yourself, if the Qanon thing is just a wacky conspiracy theory as the mainstream media professes, then why does it get so much negative attention from the left-wing press organs?

Below I am sharing a link to a 13-minute introductory video about the Q movement called Q – *The Plan to Save the World*. Below that link I am providing a link to an over 2,000-page book with explanations and all the Q posts as of September 2019. Presently, due to a successful attempt to silence Q, the posts have been offline for over a month. We will see whether 8Chan will be allowed by Congress to get back online. If not, you will have all the information you need to investigate further on your own if you have the interest and desire.

https://www.bitchute.com/video/D4wBENc87pqw/

Posts by Q, videos and more at the website below.

https://qmap.pub/

https://archive.org/details/QAnonBook-

You are now armed with a substantial number of information sources to start prying yourself from the fantasy world of illusion. These are not the only sources you can use to free your mind, but it is a good starting place, as well as all the books we have produced, which are listed in sequence at the end of this volume. I wish you much success on your journey if you decide to accept the challenge to free your mind from the illusions that enslave you. You have been given more than I had to start with when I embarked on my own journey. With the Q material and the Anon reporters on YouTube, humanity has been given a bit of a shortcut on this journey by providing places to focus on upcoming events, but it will still take you only part of the way. Find your courage and challenge the lies, it is your only way out of the illusion. The 'red pill' is *information*, not a magic bullet that will pull you out of the illusion. It is up to each individual to free their own mind. I have accomplished this, as have others, and it can be done, so have no fear that it is only a fool's errand to take this pathway to freedom.

# Afterword

The purpose of this book is to make the case about the fantasy world of illusion that all humanity lives in. This includes information about the major elite organizations and secret societies revealed within the pages of this book, who harbor their own brand of dastardly illusions. This book is not meant to be a comprehensive study of every aspect of the illusion. It is designed to be used as an educational springboard for those who have the courage to genuinely face the truth that hides behind the fantasy world of perceptual illusions.

At this stage of human evolution, I feel that humanity is at a crossroad. We have an opportunity to choose to release ourselves from the chains of the illusion and set a new path for a more positive future for subsequent generations, or we can choose to continue on as humanity has through all past ages, developing technological toys while our consciousness sits rotting and stagnant in the first cognition world of fantasy illusions. I have made my choice and have decided to move beyond the first cognition ball and chain repeating illusionary reality. To do this takes extreme fortitude and effort on the part of anyone who desires to do the same. Our books have provided the means, methods and tools for understanding how to tackle the assignment of freeing your own consciousness from the quicksand of the fantasy world of illusion.

Many people around the planet have taken the preliminary steps to remove themselves from the illusion, but they have only progressed part of the way. I tip my hat to all those who have taken these preliminary steps to free their consciousness but will also apprise them of the fact that this is a long and often wearisome journey. It will take strength, courage and determination on the part of anyone who not only starts this path, but who will see it through. Many people start the journey, but weary of it, and the quicksand of the fantasy world sucks them back into its clutches. I have seen this happen more times than I care to count. The lure of the fantasy world is one of seduction and comfort, which is the main reason that so many are lured back into its embrace. My desire is that those who read this book and our other works who decide to walk this path, ultimately succeed in their efforts. If not, I foresee a pretty grim future for humanity where the fantasy world of illusion may control humanity's consciousness for as long as it survives as a species.

# The Evolution of Consciousness Series

## Book 1

*A Philosophy for the Average Man: An Uncommon Solution to a World Without Common Sense by Endall Beall*

## Book 2

*Willful Evolution: The Path to Advanced Cognitive Awareness and a Personal Shift in Consciousness by Endall Beall*

## Book 3

*Demystifying the Mystical: Exposing Myths of the Mystical and the Supernatural by Providing Solutions to the Spirit Path and Human Evolution by Endall Beall*

## Book 4

*Navigating into the Second Cognition: The Map for your journey into higher Conscious Awareness by Endall Beall*

## Book 5

*The Energy Experience: Energy work for the Second Cognition by Mrs. Endall Beall*

## Book 6

*We Are Not Alone – Part 1: Advancing Cognitive Awareness in an Interactive Universe by Endall Beall*


## Book 7

*We Are Not Alone – Part 2: Advancing Cognitive Awareness through Historical Revelations - Endall Beall*


## Book 8

*Advanced Teachings for the Second Cognition by Mrs. Endall Beall*


## Book 9

*We Are Not Alone – Part 3: The Luciferian Agenda of the Mother Goddess by Endall Beall*

# Companion Volumes to The Evolution of Consciousness Series

*False Prophecies, Reassessing Buddha and the Call to the Second Cognition by Endall Beall*

*Operator's Manual for the True Spirit Warrior by Endall Beall*

*Spiritual Pragmatism: A Practical Approach to Spirit Work in a World Controlled by Ego by Endall Beall*

*Revamping Psychology: A Critique of Transpersonal Psychology Viewed From the Second Cognition by Endall Beall & Mrs. Endall Beall*

*The Common Sense Revolution: Creating Common Ground and Genuine Common Sense – Endall Beall and the Psoyca Crew (2016)*

# Second Cognition Series

## Book 1

*The New Paradigm Transcripts: Teachings for a New Tomorrow by Endall Beall & Doug Michael*

## Book 2

*Breaking the Chains of the First Cognition: Tools for Understanding the Path to the Second Cognition by Endall Beall & Doug Michael*

## Book 3

*PSOYCA – Road to the Second Cognition by Endall Beall & Doug Michael*

## Book 4

*The Energetic War Against Humanity: The 6,000 Year War Against Human Cognitive Advancement by Endall Beall*

## Book 5

*The Cognitive Illusion of History: How Humanity Has Been Controlled Through Selective and Biased Historical Reporting by Endall Beall & Doug Michael*

## Book 6

*The Second Cognition Toolbox: Requirements for Advancing Your Consciousness by Endall Beall*

## Book 7

*Firestarters: The Gemma and Endall Transcripts – by Endall Beall and Gemma Beall*

## Book 8

*No Trespassing: Creating a New World Based on Mutual Respect by Endall Beall*

## Book 9

*Psoyca Consciousness by Endall Beall*

## Companion Volumes to the Second Cognition Series

*Understanding Wisdom: A Treatise on Wisdom Viewed from the Second Cognition by Endall Beall*

*From Belief to Truth – From Truth to Wisdom by Endall Beall*

*The Psychology of Becoming Human: Evolving Beyond Psychological Conditioning by Endall Beall*

## Standalone Work: Available for free .pdf download at our website

*Clarifying the don Juan Teachings for the Second Cognition: A Pragmatic Reanalysis Without the Mystical Misdirection – by Endall Beall*

Free pdf download of this book at the link below

https://www.demystifyingthemystical.com/#/book/17

# Beyond Second Cognition Series

## Book 1

*Gutting Mysticism: Explaining the Roots of All Supernatural Belief by Endall Beall (2018) by Endall Beall*

## Book 2

*Religion, the Goddess and the Mind Virus of Heaven: The Deception of Holiness in Human Belief Systems (2018) by Endall Beall*

## Book 3

*Introduction to the Multiverse: The Layman's Guide to the Cosmos (2018) by Endall Beall*

## Book 4

*Facing the Truth: Conspiracy or Plan? 100 Years of Subversive Psychological Warfare Against America (2018) by Endall Beall*

## Book 5

*The No Rules Multiverse: The Endeavor to Repair a Faulty Creation (2019) by Endall Beall*

## Companion Volumes to Beyond Second Cognition Series

*Emotionalism: How the Human Herds are Controlled (2019) by Endall Beall*

*The Truth About the 'Divine' Soul: The Late Creation of the Concept of Heaven (2019) by Endall Beall*

*Challenging Philosophy and the Philosophers: Explaining Nietzsche to Academic Philosophers (2019) by Endall Beall*

*Fantasy World: Humanity's Avoidance of the Truth to Live in a World of Illusion (2019) by Endall Beall*

For questions or inquiries contact the authors at *http://demystifyingthemystical.com/#/*

Further work by these authors can be found at the Gemma Beall YouTube channel at
https://www.youtube.com/channel/UCN3VfiNrozRSUBiDIR8k9EA

Or through the Gemma Beall Patreon channel for subscriptions of $5 per month for access to 300 video presentation, and $7 per month for all the videos and an expanding number of educational podcasts, chapter previews, blogs and an interactive comment forum.
https://www.patreon.com/GemmaBeall/

Made in the USA
Columbia, SC
26 September 2019